GREAT WAR BRITAIN
COVENTRY
Remembering 1914-18

GREAT WAR BRITAIN

COVENTRY

Remembering 1914–18

PETER WALTERS

The
History
Press

In memory of my grandfathers

C.J. Walters (11th Hussars)
J.L. Sheldon (Essex Regiment)

Soldiers of the Great War

First published 2016

The History Press
The Mill, Brimscombe Port
Stroud, Gloucestershire, GL5 2QG
www.thehistorypress.co.uk

British Library Cataloguing in Publication Data.
A catalogue record for this book is available from the British Library.

ISBN 978 0 7509 6075 5

Typesetting and origination by The History Press
Printed in Malta by Melita Press

CONTENTS

TIMELINE

1914

28 June

*Assassination of Archduke
Franz Ferdinand in Sarajevo*

4 August

Great Britain declares war on Germany

5 August

*7th Battalion, Royal Warwickshire
Regiment leaves Coventry for war service*

23 August

Battle of Tannenberg commences

6 September

First Battle of the Marne

8 September

*Coventry's German-born Mayor, Siegfried
Bettmann, announces his resignation*

7 October

Arrival of Belgian refugees in Coventry

19 October

First Battle of Ypres

1915

15 March

*Royal Munster Fusiliers leave
Coventry for the Dardenelles*

25 April

Allied landing at Gallipoli

7 May

Germans torpedo and sink the Lusitania

31 May

*First Coventry-built plane
flown to Farnborough*

31 May

*First German Zeppelin
raid on London*

22 July

*King George V visits Coventry
to inspect munitions factories*

20 December

*Allies complete evacuations and
withdraw from Gallipoli*

1916

10 January

*Public lighting restrictions
imposed in Coventry*

24 January

*The British Government
introduces conscription*

21 February

Battle of Verdun commences

31 May

Battle of Jutland

4 June

Brusilov Offensive commences

1 July

*First day of the Battle of the Somme,
which claims 57,000 British casualties*

27 August

Italy declares war on Germany

18 December

Battle of Verdun ends

1917

6 April

United States declares war on Germany

9 April

Battle of Arras

31 July

Third Battle of Ypres (Passchendaele)

20 August

Third Battle of Verdun

18 September

*Queen Mary visits White and
Poppe works in Coventry*

26 October

Second Battle of Passchendaele

17 November

*Coventry munitions workers
strike over food shortages*

20 November

Battle of Cambrai

7 December

USA declares war on Austria-Hungary

1918

12 January

Coventry VC Arthur Hutt receives civic welcome

10 February

Tank Week starts in Coventry

3 March

Russia and the Central Powers sign the Treaty of Brest-Litovsk

21 March

Second Battle of the Somme

12 April

Zeppelin bombs fall on outskirts of Coventry

15 July

Second Battle of the Marne

8 August

Battle of Amiens, first stage of the Hundred Days Offensive

22 September

Allied victory in the Balkans

27 September

Storming of the Hindenburg Line

8 November

Armistice negotiations commence

9 November

Kaiser Wilhelm II abdicates, Germany is declared a Republic

11 November

Armistice Day, cessation of hostilities on Western Front

About the Author

Peter Walters is a freelance writer and has written widely about the history of Coventry. He lives in the city and is an active member of the local heritage campaigning group, The Coventry Society. His first book, *The Story of Coventry*, was published by The History Press in 2013.

ACKNOWLEDGEMENTS

I am hugely indebted to the following people, without whose knowledge, support and enthusiasm the story of Coventry in the First World War would have remained a closed book to me: Jim Brown, Carolyn Ewing, David Fry, Chris Holland, Huw Jones, Damien Kimberley, Mark Radford, Keith Railton, Terry Reeves, Martin Roberts and Brian Stote.

Church folk on the march while in Sarajevo an assassin's bullet triggers the First World War.

COURTESY OF DAVID FRY

INTRODUCTION

On a summer Sunday morning, bathed in brilliant sunshine, the parishioners and clergy of St John the Baptist, one of Coventry's oldest churches, marched through the streets in joyful procession to mark their annual saint's day.

More than a thousand miles away, at the other end of Europe, an assassin's bullet was ending the life of Archduke Franz Ferdinand, heir to the Habsburg empire. The date was 28 June 1914. Within six weeks Europe was at war, with millions of men mobilised and marching towards a conflagration the scale of which the world had never before seen.

Yet that summer in Coventry thoughts were far from fatal alliances and the collapse of empires. It was a city of the young, with more people under the age of 20 than over it, and they were intent on having a good time.

High wages in a city that had pioneered both the bicycle and the automobile industries had fuelled a boom in shops and places of entertainment. Earnings, wrote one disapproving Coventry clergyman, were being 'too largely expended on crude and trivial satisfaction'.

In this heady boom town, local concerns focused on congestion – too many motor cars for the narrow medieval thoroughfares of the old city and not enough homes for a population that had exploded since the turn of the century, mostly with young, able-bodied immigrants drawn from bigger cities like London and Birmingham in search of that good life.

The fashionable girl about town in Coventry.

COURTESY OF MARK RADFORD

Radford Garden Suburb, Coventry's first serious response to crippling housing shortages, had been officially launched in June 1914, with plans for 200 homes on a 14-acre site. In late July councillors nodded through a £300,000 road-building project for two new city centre streets, Corporation Street and Trinity Street, that would ease traffic congestion and sweep away clusters of medieval buildings described by one prominent member of the council as 'germ breeding houses'.

If there was a niggling worry amongst those who were thinking beyond their next payday it concerned Ireland, where on 23 July thousands of hard-line Protestants had flocked to take up arms in defiance of the government's proposals for Home Rule.

The Austrian ultimatum to Serbia, delivered on the same day, caused barely a ripple, even to a British Government still confident that it could stay out of any conflicts on the Continent. As late as 2 August, Prime Minister Herbert Asquith was assuring the German ambassador in London that Britain would not intervene, as long as his country didn't invade Belgium.

By that Sunday night more than 25,000 of Coventry's residents, revelling in the new-found excitement of proper industrial holidays, had already left by train for what promised to be a dazzling Bank Holiday weekend at their favourite seaside resorts in North Wales and Lancashire.

The city they would return to days later, a little punch-drunk at the speed of events, was destined to become one of the powerhouses of Britain's war effort, a munitions centre labelled the 'busiest town in Britain' and compared by *The Times* newspaper in 1916 to the US industrial dynamo that was Detroit.

Not for the first, nor the last time in its history, Coventry was on the brink of seismic change.

Peter Walters, 2016

1

OUTBREAK OF WAR

To more feverish imaginations it might have seemed like a destructive omen of the conflict to come.

As Coventry journalist Henry Wilkins and his wife knelt in prayer during the Sunday service at Holy Trinity, the peace of the fourteenth-century church was shattered by two loud crashes as heavy stonework detached itself from the south face of the tower and fell on to the roof of the organ loft.

Nobody was hurt and in his *Journal of the European War*, Wilkins recorded the incident, on the morning of 2 August 1914, without comment. Yet by then other prominent Coventry citizens already knew that the die for war had been cast.

The day before, Siegfried Bettmann, the city's German-born Mayor and the founder of the Triumph Company, had called an urgent meeting of Coventry's biggest manufacturers at the request of representatives from the War Office.

As they discussed motorcycle production, Bettmann asked a senior official where all the machines they required were to be used. He was told Belgium and at that moment, he wrote later, he knew that the fate of Europe was sealed.

AN ALIEN MENACE

The first wild rumour of the war swept through Coventry during the night of 4 August, as Britain's ultimatum to Germany ran out. The German Army, it reported, had landed at Flamborough Head in Yorkshire and was marching south towards the Midlands. Distant rumbles and flashes of light in the sky were evidence that a major defensive battle was taking place somewhere to the north-east.

It turned out to be simply a distant thunderstorm but the sinister interpretation placed upon it was evidence of the jumpiness infecting many now that conflict was a reality.

Within four days, Ministers had rushed through the Aliens Restriction Act, which required people of German extraction to register with the police. In Coventry that initially meant around seventy individuals, mostly shopkeepers and hotel staff.

In theory at least, this new regulation also applied to Coventry's Mayor and the Triumph Company founder, the Nuremberg-born Siegfried Bettmann. He had become a naturalised Briton in the 1890s, taken an English wife and was, in his own words, 'proud to be an Englishman, not only by law, but by marriage and sentiment'.

This most patriotic and loyal of Coventrians was suddenly a target for smear and innuendo. A group of 'loyal' citizens had petitioned the Home Office for his instant removal as Mayor, a request that was turned down, but the Foreign Office did decree that he should not serve a second year as Mayor, as custom dictated, when his first term ended in November.

Nationally, anti-German sentiment, stoked up by rabble-rousers like the swindler Horatio Bottomley and his *John Bull* weekly magazine, quickly caught Bettmann in its snare.

The *London Evening News* ran a story that German investors held almost all of the Triumph Company's £130,000 capital. It was a lie for which its sister paper, *The Times*, later had to issue a public apology. But the damage had been done. Bettmann, embittered by the lack of trust shown in him, announced on 8 September that he would be stepping down when his term of office ended on 9 November.

German-born Siegfried Bettmann, proud to be English.

What War?

Bettmann's prescience did not extend to Coventry's newspapers. For weeks, the distant rumble of impending hostilities had been largely ignored in favour of the hustle and bustle of summer fêtes and company sports days.

The city's evening newspaper, *The Midland Daily Telegraph*, had reported the death of Franz Ferdinand in its 29 June edition under the headline 'Austrian Tragedy'. But it had not commented on the growing tensions across Europe until mid-July and even as peace finally came to a shuddering halt, at 11 p.m. on the night of Monday 4 August, there was the sense of a story missed.

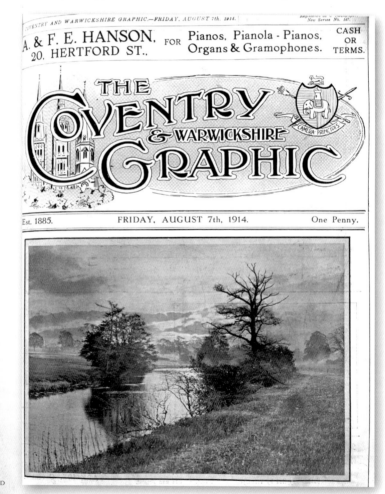

COVENTRY AND WARWICKSHIRE GRAPHIC.—FRIDAY, AUGUST 7th, 1914.   New Series No. 147.

A. & F. E. HANSON, 20, HERTFORD ST., FOR Pianos, Pianola - Pianos, Organs & Gramophones. CASH OR TERMS.

THE Coventry & WARWICKSHIRE GRAPHIC

Est. 1885.   FRIDAY, AUGUST 7th, 1914.   One Penny.

The first front page of the war — a Warwickshire scene at sunset.

COURTESY OF MARK RADFORD

On the following day the paper, its front page purely advertising, as usual, led its news columns inside with the curiously downbeat headline 'Great Britain has declared war on Germany. That is the vital fact of today's news.'

The weekly *Coventry Herald*, making its first appearance of the war on 7 August, commented somewhat belatedly, 'Coventry has never passed through such a thrilling week as the present one has been.' Its chief rival, the *Coventry Graphic*, published on the same day, was almost word for word. 'Never before in living memory,' it declared, 'has Coventry experienced such a week of sensations as this Bank Holiday week.'

It was as if the war had simply stolen up on everybody.

At the turn of the twentieth century, Coventry was still recognisably an old weaving town, with a population of just under 70,000. By the outbreak of the First World War its new industries had swelled that figure to 114,000, and by 1918 it had reached 142,000, making it the country's fastest growing urban centre.

Marching to War

For the Territorials of the 7th Royal Warwickshire Regiment, a battalion full of Coventry men, the Bank Holiday weekend had begun with a journey by train to their annual summer training camp at Rhyl in North Wales. There, they were still waiting for some of their equipment to arrive when orders were received to turn around, return to Coventry and prepare for mobilisation.

Marching to war. Coventry says farewell to its Territorials.

COURTESY OF THE
HERBERT HISTORY CENTRE

They spent the night of 4 August, as war was being declared, at the city's Drill Hall in Queen Victoria Road, where, as the news broke around midnight, crowds gathered to sing 'Rule Britannia' and 'Three Cheers for the Red, White and Blue' in an outpouring of patriotic excitement.

The battalion left Coventry the following evening, marching to the railway station through streets lined with cheering crowds, despite official attempts to keep its time of departure a secret.

Eyewitness accounts in the newspapers spoke of 'stirring and memorable scenes' as, shortly after 7 p.m., the battalion band struck up the light infantry march 'Sons of the Brave' and led the 850 men of the 7th Royal Warwickshire Regiment up Warwick Road to the railway station to two special trains that were to take them south, to war. One correspondent wrote:

> Attracted by the pulsing music of the band, people rushed breathlessly from every direction to swell the throng and lend their voices to ringing farewell cheers which were given. Windows of the houses on the route were hastily thrown open and handkerchiefs waved. Women and girls – mothers, wives, sisters and sweethearts – hastened along the side of the ranks bidding encouraging and cheering farewells to their loved ones.

That same evening, the men and horses of C Section, Warwickshire Royal Horse Artillery, left their base at the city's Smithford Street barracks and took the road to Leamington to meet up with their comrades in other Warwickshire batteries. Within a week, the 4th South Midland Howitzer Brigade, Royal Field Artillery, another unit with many Coventry men in it, had followed the Territorials to the railway station.

The public farewell given to these later military departures was more muted. Coventry never had a Pals Battalion in the infantry, as such, but the part-time soldiers of the 7th Battalion, Royal Warwickshire Regiment were as close as the city got to one.

Nor did cheering crowds gather to see off up to a thousand Coventry reservists – former servicemen being recalled to the

Kitchener's call to arms.

August 21st, 1914.   *THE COVENTRY GRAPHIC.*   113

YOUR KING & COUNTRY NEED YOU.

A CALL TO ARMS.

An addition of 100,000 men to his Majesty's regular Army are immediately necessary in the present grave National emergency.

Lord Kitchener is confident that this appeal will be at once responded to by all those who have the safety of our Empire at heart.

TERMS OF SERVICE.

General service for a period of three years or until the war is concluded.

Age of enlistment between 19 and 30.

HOW TO JOIN.

Full information can be obtained at any post office in the kingdom, or at any military depot.

GOD SAVE THE KING!

colours – who in the first week of the war slipped away in ones and twos to rejoin their regiment or their ship. But there was an awareness that these men in particular were husbands and fathers and that their families must be looked after.

In stirring words, local newspapers recalled the public's generosity during the South African War fifteen years earlier, when a Reservists Fund, largely raised by the working men of the city, had supported many families in their hour of need. And they called on the well-to-do and the middle classes to get involved this time too:

Our citizen soldiers have taken the rifle to defend us. Our reservists have gone back to their posts in the regiment and the battleship in our interest as much as, if not more than, their own.

What of the mothers and wives and children which so many of them have left behind in humble little homes in our city? Their welfare must be a sacred charge upon others. If we allow the helpless dependants of these our fellow men to fall into grinding poverty and lack any of the common comforts of life, we shall show ourselves less than men.

Mayor Bettmann was quick to show leadership, making a passionate speech in support of the Prince of Wales' national war fund, but also raising more than £6,000 in quick time for his own Mayoral relief fund, resisting the government's preference for every fund-raising effort to be routed through the national body. Over the course of the war this local fund would raise more than £100,000 for the dependants of Coventry's fighting men.

The War at Home

To forestall a run on the banks, the Asquith government's first action was to extend the Bank Holiday until Friday 8 August, thereby depriving many of Coventry's manufacturing companies of the funds they needed to put in a highly productive week.

In an atmosphere of intensifying war fever, 200 Boy Scouts, somewhat bizarrely, were deployed to guard important installations such as the gas works, electricity substations, telegraph lines and the Coventry Canal. Local industrialists, led by machine tool manufacturer Alfred Herbert, set about raising a local defence force, a move that was quickly abandoned when the government made its disapproval known. Instead, Coventry's Chief Constable, Charles Charsley, was given permission to recruit up to 600 special constables as enlistment began to thin his own ranks.

The Triumph of "Culture."

The above fine cartoon, which we are privileged to reproduce from "Punch," indicates how the boasted culture and education of Germany has proved to be only a veneer over brutal savagery, which has found expression in the appalling atrocities reported from Belgium.

The enemy, as seen by Punch.

The citizen newly at war was not short of official advice, as the government took space in *The Times*, followed up in many local papers, to offer some ground rules under the heading of 'How to be useful: The duty of citizens':

> First and foremost, keep your heads. Be calm. Go about your ordinary business quietly and soberly. Do not indulge in excitement or foolish demonstrations. Explain to the young and ignorant what war is and why we have been forced to wage it.
>
> Do not store goods and create an artificial scarcity to the hurt of others. Remember that it is an act of mean and selfish cowardice.

The medical magazine *The Lancet* joined in, urging its well-to-do readers to cut down on household expenses, but not to get rid of the servants.

In Coventry, the anti-hoarding message was reinforced by the Mayor, who called on wealthier citizens not to plunder food shops at the cost of the poor, an issue that would have dramatic consequences in the city later in the war. But by the time Mayor Bettmann spoke out, a run on foods like flour, sugar, bacon, oatmeal, tinned meats, tea and coffee had already caused many shopkeepers to run out of stock and close.

Despite reassurances given to the *Coventry Herald* newspaper by the manager of one large provisions store – that as long as the Royal Navy could keep trade routes open, there was no need for food prices to increase – it was already happening.

In the second week of August the government felt obliged to issue a guide to maximum food prices nationally. It capped sugar at 3*s* ¾*d* a pound, imported butter at 1*s* 6*d*, British bacon at 1*s* 3*d* and colonial cheese at 9*s* ½*d*.

It also announced its intention to introduce a standard loaf which was quickly, and not fondly, dubbed War Bread. This was not the soft white bread the public was used to, but was a coarser, wholemeal loaf, which was much healthier, but more importantly less costly in terms of imported flour.

Britain's own harvest in 1914 had looked promising, but in the early weeks of the war there was considerable disquiet that recruiting for the army would draw too many men off the land, leaving many women and the elderly physically unable to get in the harvest.

Government agents were also active in the streets and on the farms, buying up horses for the Continental campaign to come and in some cases literally taking them from between the shafts of carts as they went about their daily work. Without horses, farmers complained, how could they get in oats that had already been cut and the rapidly ripening barley and wheat harvests?

Opposition to War

At the outbreak of war, it was reported that so-called Passive Resisters in Coventry had fallen in number from eighty to around ten, but there were influential voices raised locally who had grave misgivings about the conflict.

Coventry's Liberal MP David Marshall Mason.
COURTESY OF DAVID FRY

Coventry's Liberal MP David Marshall Mason, who had succeeded his namesake the novelist A.E.W. Mason in 1910, had for months been opposing naval spending in Parliament, in defiance of his own Liberal government.

A banker by profession, Mason made himself a one-man awkward squad in the House of Commons, voting against the government more than thirty times in the early months of 1914. On the eve of war, he claimed that the idea of Germany attacking Britain was nonsense, suggesting that spending on the army and the navy should be cut, not increased.

Accused of not supporting the govern-ment in a crisis, he was attacked by the national press in a campaign orchestrated,

it was said, by some of the big players in the munitions industry, including Coventry Ordnance Works.

Reluctantly, he came to acknowledge that his trust in Germany had been misplaced. In a letter to his Coventry political agent in mid-August, he wrote, 'This was a bad business, but there appears to have been no doubt that Germany did wrong and she ought, and probably will, suffer for it. We must present a united front to the enemy.'

Mason would go on to become an important figure in the peace movement in Britain between the two world wars. But the electors of Coventry never did understand his point of view and when Parliamentary elections resumed in 1918, he had to run as an Independent Liberal. He finished last in a field of five to the Conservative Edward Manville, who was chairman of the Daimler Company.

P.E.T. Widdrington, vicar of St Peter's church in Hillfields.
COURTESY OF DAVID FRY

Another who expressed strong reservations about the war was the influential Christian Socialist vicar of St Peter's church in Hillfields, the Revd Percy Elborough Tinling Widdrington.

A genuine friend to the working man, Widdrington reluctantly came to support war with Germany as a national obligation that could not be honourably evaded, but passed up no opportunity to press for better conditions in the munitions factories. In May 1917 he told a national Christian Socialist conference that it was becoming impossible for munitions workers to take any rest as the pressure on them to make money was too strong.

He was much loved for it. When he left Coventry in 1918, trade unionists presented him with an illuminated address as a man who had been to them 'an inspiration and a guide whom they could follow with confidence'.

More forceful in his opposition to the war was Richard 'Dick' Wallhead, who had been adopted as the Independent Labour Party's (ILP) candidate for Coventry in 1912.

Wallhead, a decorator turned journalist and lecturer, had a way with words and was not frightened to court controversy.

In a speech in the city in October 1914, he claimed that there were 'pig holes' in the north of England that were worse than anything seen in Germany; that the government of France was utterly corrupt and that, by contrast, Germany's administration was admirable. Views like these were to earn Wallhead a prison sentence for sedition later in the war and those who shared them in the ILP were careful to keep their heads down, certainly for the first two years of the conflict.

Doing Their Bit

Appeals for the able-bodied young men of Coventry to put King and Country first and join up were in all the local newspapers before the first week of the war was out. By 21 August nearly 400 men had answered Lord Kitchener's call and enlisted at Coventry's new recruiting office, set up in the city's Masonic Hall in Little Park Street.

Waiting six hours in the sun to join up.
COURTESY OF MARK RADFORD

By the end of the month, the figure was running at more than a hundred a day, despite a patently inadequate system that could not process them fast enough and left many sweltering in a queue for up to six hours in blazing sunshine as they waited to join up. Some went home in frustration and left the city to enlist elsewhere.

Unsurprisingly perhaps, in a city of engineers, there was a lot of interest in the army engineers and in the 'flying sections' of the army, already officially known as the Royal Flying Corps. Sadly those manning the recruiting station had not been instructed to recruit for that area of the military and would-be flyers and flight engineers found themselves in infantry regiments.

Among those young men who might be counted as Coventry's sporting elite, the pressure to join up was intense. In early September, Coventry Rugby Club suspended its fixture list and urged its players to enlist, telling them that 'their athletic training particularly qualifies them for the service of their country'.

Professional football stumbled on through the first months of the war, criticised in some quarters as unpatriotic, but so many players had joined up that by early 1915 it fizzled out. Struggling Coventry City played their final home game in April, fearful that after relegation from Division 1 of the Southern League in 1914, they might not be able to resurrect the club when the time came.

The war was to take a toll on these Coventry sportsmen. One casualty was Coventry Rugby Club's former England international Will Oldham, seriously wounded in September 1915 while serving with the Warwickshire Yeomanry. Six Coventry City footballers were to lose their lives in the war, including Steve Jackson, who had signed for the club in 1911, enlisted in September 1914, won the Military Medal as a sergeant in the South Staffordshire Regiment and was killed in October 1917.

Cricket, the other closely followed team game in the city, suffered too. At the end of June in one of their last important matches, Coventry and North Warwickshire, the city's premier cricket club, had

> Despite its crowded nature, Coventry in 1914 had a remarkably low death rate for an industrial city. Standing at 11.4 per thousand head of population, it was far lower than many of the wealthier surrounding towns, a fact attributed to the presence of so many able-bodied young men who could afford decent accommodation and plentiful food.

W.OLDHAM
COVENTRY.F.C

faced a Warwickshire county eleven. Batting at number three for the Coventry side was Reginald George Pridmore, from a well-known city family, who'd been a hockey gold medallist at the 1908 Olympics.

As Major Pridmore of the Royal Field Artillery, he was to lose his life on the battlefields of France. As was the man who bowled him for thirty-nine that day, Percy Jeeves, later of the 15th Royal Warwickshire Regiment, who posthumously gave his name to novelist P.G. Wodehouse's most celebrated character.

Industry's Response

For Coventry's manufacturing companies the initial rush to the recruiting office was problematic. The speed with which war had come had left many of them, particularly those with a strong export business, struggling to cope with new uncertainties, and now they faced losing whole chunks of their workforce.

Caught between patriotism and business, they reacted in different ways. While the machine tool firm Alfred Herbert took space in local papers to 'request all workmen who are willing to resume work to hand in their names in case their services may be required', the vehicle maker Siddeley-Deasy paraded its workforce in front of its Parkside factory, gave them a formal discharge and ordered them to join up. Within days the company had received an order for 150 lorries and was desperately trying to have them recalled.

Another of Coventry's major employers, the artificial silk manufacturer Courtaulds, claimed that it had contributed the equivalent of a whole company of Territorials to the 7th Battalion, Royal Warwicks, while cycle company Rudge Whitworth and car maker Daimler each estimated they had lost hundreds of men immediately to mobilisation.

On the day that war was declared, Coventry's daily paper, *The Midland Daily Telegraph*, carried a string of adverts from companies offering cash loans for the holidays, the 1914 equivalent of payday lenders. 'Borrow from an Englishman', proclaimed one, desperately seeking a patriotic angle.

Daimler, already the industrial company by which others liked to measure themselves, had not let the loss of 221 employees who were Reservists or Territorials hold it back. Within a week more than a hundred of its cars and lorries had been commandeered by the War Office for use as ambulances and staff cars, and the company was scouring its own showrooms nationwide to double that figure.

In 1910 Daimler had begun manufacturing motor omnibuses, an increasingly popular form of public transport that by the outbreak of war was spreading rapidly across the country. Coventry had been one of the first local authorities to acquire a fleet of its own; the first service between the city and Birmingham began at the end of March 1914. And as demand for vehicles in France grew, it was

Daimlers in Ostend on their way to the war.
COURTESY OF MARK RADFORD

reported that ten Daimler buses a week were being shipped from the streets of London to the front line.

Such was the high profile of the company's vehicles in France early in the war that His Royal Highness the Prince of Wales (later King Edward VIII) exclaimed on a visit to the front, 'It seems to me that the Daimler people are running this war.'

Daimler went on to become one of the most innovative and productive of Coventry's major munitions and armaments manufacturers, producing more vehicle chassis than any other firm, playing a key role in the development of the tank and turning its hand successfully to aircraft building.

Yet it also showed a broader understanding of the needs of its wartime workforce, by 1916 setting up a canteen at its Sandy Lane works that was capable of serving 1,300 meals a day, introducing a concert programme organised by the workers themselves, and giving women workers restrooms where they could recover if they felt overwrought or were suffering from a nervous breakdown.

Daimler also demonstrated an awareness of international issues, offering work in its tool room to a new group of citizens seeking sanctuary in Coventry.

The Belgian Refugees

Trying to protect 'gallant little Belgium' was the aim that led Britain into the war, and it wasn't long before Asquith's government was being asked to give shelter to 50,000 refugees from that battered country.

In Coventry, a Belgian Relief Fund raised more than £2,000 within weeks, its chief means of raising money a series of public lectures on subjects including 'Causes of The War' and 'Belgium Before and After the German Invasion'.

The city's outgoing Mayor, Siegfried Bettmann, was instrumental in arranging for Whitley Abbey, a large unused house belonging to the Petre family, to be made habitable and opened up as accommodation for Belgian refugees. An appeal for furniture and household equipment was swiftly answered and the first party of twenty-two arrived from London on 7 October; three families described as a 'nice class of work people'.

Within days another group of married couples and business people followed, although one couple proved so rude and ungrateful for the help they were receiving that they were sent back to London and placed under police supervision on suspicion of being German.

The first party of Belgian refugees at Whitley Abbey.
COURTESY OF MARK RADFORD

By the end of the month there were 120 Belgians living at Whitley Abbey, the advance guard for more than 1,700 people who were to make their home in Coventry in the years up to 1918, many in lodgings around the city. Local people, often bearing gifts, were allowed to visit them at the abbey on Thursday and Saturday afternoons, although a limit of a hundred visitors a day had to be quickly imposed to control numbers.

By the spring of 1915 there were several dozen Belgian children in city schools. Wheatley Street School alone was said to have thirty-seven on its books. Daimler was not the only company to offer work to their fathers, but led the way with a special department set up to deal with them, employing up to 150 Belgian workers at any one time. They received equal treatment to their British workmates and had access to the company's insurance scheme.

None of this seems to have sparked resentment among Coventry workers, partly because as the war effort locally cranked into gear there was more work than could be handled. Firms were careful to ensure that jobs for Belgian refugees would not imperil local prospects.

All of which led to sincere expressions of gratitude, even before hostilities had ended. In July 1918, a memorial tablet expressing Belgium's thanks to Coventry was unveiled in St Mary's Hall by the Belgian Consul-General in Britain, Monsieur Edouard Pollet. In 1920 the King of the Belgians awarded commemorative medals to Coventry couple Charles and Evelyn Mast, who had supervised the reception given to the refugees.

Getting Home

In the first weeks of war, Coventry had its own refugees to worry about – local people caught abroad on the Continent by the rapid pace of events as the German armies swept through Belgium into France.

The city's Town Clerk, George Sutton, made it safely back from holiday in Switzerland, as did the daughter of the journalist Henry Wilkins, who had been on a short trip to Belgium. But others were not so fortunate.

Edgar Bainton, son of the Revd George Bainton, Minister of West Orchard Wesleyan chapel, was taken into custody in Frankfurt with his wife Ethel as they tried to make their way home from the Wagner Festival in Bayreuth. Ethel was allowed to return to England in a party of repatriated women, but Edgar was interned in a civilian detention camp near Berlin, where he remained until March 1918 when his health began to deteriorate and he was sent to The Hague to recover.

A musical prodigy who had made his first public appearance as a pianist at the age of 9, Bainton later emigrated to Australia where he become one of that country's most important composers of church music.

The war had also begun to break what had been close ties between the British and German people, at many levels. Among those swept up by the government's Aliens Restriction Act and taken to an internment camp at Newbury were a number of German waiters working at the city's best hotel, the King's Head, while in mid-August it was reported that the popular Adelmann family of musicians from Germany would no longer be appearing, as arranged, at the Coventry Hippodrome.

At another level, a correspondent to the *Coventry Graphic* who had spent fifteen years living in Germany expressed sympathy for its people. 'The fault lies entirely with the military caste,' he wrote, 'who have exercised a dominance in Germany such as we cannot imagine in Britain. The German people, who no more wanted war than we did, will suffer economically and physically.'

2

Preparations at Home

By the beginning of September, more than a thousand men had passed through Coventry's recruiting centre at the Masonic Hall on Little Park Street.

Staff numbers had been trebled and the whole building turned over to the business of assessing and signing up the able-bodied young men of the city, but there were still queues out into the street, giving newspaper reporters the opportunity to do a little patriotic drum-beating themselves. 'A glance at the groups shows that the men are of the best sort,' reported the *Coventry Herald*, 'and it's evident that every sector of the community is yielding its quota of recruits.'

Made of the right stuff.
COURTESY OF MARK RADFORD

Rousing cheers, the paper reported, greeted successful applicants when the results of their physical examinations were known. It picked out for special mention sixty-two employees of the Siddeley-Deasy company, who had marched in formation from the factory down to the recruiting office.

The general mood of excitement was voiced by one would-be soldier, still dressed as a clerk, who was overheard to say, 'I hope we don't get kept in a barrack-yard drilling all the time and never have a chance at having a slap at the barbarians.' An older man standing in the queue, a grizzled veteran who'd been wounded in the Boer War, responded, 'These here Germans will not be so easily licked. They've been shot down like rabbits and there's millions of them.'

Within a month, the gloss had begun to wear off enlistment and the recruiting figures had slowed. There were complaints that Coventry was not now pulling its weight when it came to providing men for the war and in early October, when a new wave of recruits to the Royal Warwickshire Regiment marched to the railway station without any form of public send-off, there was outrage in the newspapers.

In truth, the city's employers might have had a hand in encouraging this slump in recruitment, as they were beginning to show an unwillingness to allow their most skilled employees to join up, preferring them instead to stay behind on war work. It was an uncomfortable dilemma for many people in Coventry that for the duration of the war never entirely resolved itself.

Protecting Old Coventry

One area of recruitment that was going well, however, was for Coventry's new City Guild, a conservation society formed earlier in the year 'to take practical and legitimate steps to prevent as far as possible the further destruction of ancient buildings in the city of Coventry'.

The City Guild reflected a growing concern among those with family roots in Coventry who saw their historic city being swept away by youthful incomers with no sense of its rich and colourful past.

Historic buildings in Gosford Street make way for the giant Hotchkiss works.
COURTESY OF MARK RADFORD

The original Council House scheme, with shops at street level.
COURTESY OF DAVID FRY

Led by an influential group of women, including the city historian Mary Dormer Harris and the girls' school novelist Angela Brazil, it determined that its first task was to schedule the old houses of the city, especially those that were likely to change hands.

The first building to attract its active concern was the city's rundown but achingly historic Palace Yard, which had recently come on to the market. The City Guild was quick too to voice its opposition to the destruction of ancient streets for the traffic-relieving

Trinity Street and Corporation Street, although in the end it was the government that put a stop to that by forbidding local authorities to carry out major town improvement schemes in time of war.

But it was already too late to protect some of Coventry's most appealing medieval houses, cleared some years before to make way for the city's new Council House in Earl Street, which was nearing completion in the autumn of 1914. The new council headquarters, built at a cost of just over £60,000, had attracted general approval, apart from the corner-piece clock tower, widely regarded as being 'too stubby' for a building with a 280ft-long frontage.

First Casualties

A month of hearsay despatches from rumoured battlefields ended in early September with the arrival of the first wounded soldiers in Coventry. Among them were two city men from the 1st Battalion, Royal Warwickshire Regiment, wounded in the same action.

Private Andrew Townsend from the Stoke area of Coventry had received a rifle bullet in his calf during the fighting around Mons and while carrying him to the rear, Bandsman Sidney Carter from Hillfields, acting as a stretcher-bearer, had been struck by shrapnel in the thigh and had to crawl three-quarters of a mile to a casualty station.

Carter's first-hand account of an earlier brush with the enemy, given to a local newspaper at a time before army censors put a block on such vivid combat stories, spared no lurid detail.

On the march somewhere between Mons and Cambrai, he reported, the 1,100 men of the battalion had been digging in when they were attacked by a force of Uhlans, German cavalrymen with a reputation for brutality, who, he claimed, were wearing French uniforms and driving women and children before them.

The Royal Warwicks drove them off with heavy casualties but had suffered badly themselves in a series of clashes with the enemy in the chaos of the fighting retreat from Mons. Carter claimed he saw an officer with an arm severed still directing his men and said he witnessed a soldier reel 6 or 7 yards, like a drunken man, with his head blown off.

Private Sidney Carter, a man with a tale to tell.
COURTESY OF MARK RADFORD

True or not, accounts like this were beginning to bring home the grim reality of the war. When news leaked out that the first convoy of wounded soldiers, carrying twenty men with head and arm wounds, was expected at Coventry and Warwickshire Hospital, a group of onlookers gathered at the gates to cheer them in.

Wounded soldiers at Coventry and Warwickshire Hospital.

COURTESY OF THE
HERBERT HISTORY CENTRE

The hospital quickly realised that it needed to beef up its peacetime capacity of one small emergency ward and a total of 137 beds. It was helped to do so by machine tool manufacturer Alfred Herbert, already a prominent supporter of its work, who donated £1,000 to build and equip a new emergency ward for wounded soldiers in some reserve premises at the back of the main building.

The work took just ten days to complete and brought the hospital's emergency provision up to seventy beds. In the years to come it would need every one of them.

Life at Home

Among Coventry's retailers, great and small, the autumn season was traditionally the time to make money, and 1914 was shaping up to be no different.

The *Coventry Herald*, in assessing the prospects in its seasonal shopping supplement, drew a terrible contrast between autumn and war – 'golden grain and human butchery':

Here we are, almost within the range of flight of one of the death-dealing Zeppelins; but the smiling countryside of a glorious autumn in one of the loveliest counties in England does not induce serious comprehension of the actual horrors of the great campaign. Even the presence of men who have been put out of action in the firing line somehow has failed to arouse a general appreciation of what is happening.

Most people find it difficult, if not impossible, to reconcile the almost normally placid course of events at home with the devastating happenings just across the Silver Streak.

That said, the paper concluded,

… with autumn upon us, the trader is finding that business is pretty much as usual and the prospects are very good. In Coventry, shoppers have no reason whatsoever to grumble at prices. The autumn shopping season in the old city promises to be among the brightest and most successful for many years. As a shopping centre, the city takes high place among communities of like size.

A successful autumn season it may well have been, although in the Coventry Chamber of Commerce year-end report for 1914, its retail section representative, Mr V.J. Hayward, a draper with a business in White Street, did sound a note of caution. He was, he wrote, happy to report that the police had now agreed to allow cars to remain at certain specific stands in the city so that users could have more time for shopping. Concerns about parking have always signalled a certain lack of confidence among retailers.

The Chamber report as a whole was very bullish about business in Coventry that autumn, informing members that 'the effect of the war on Coventry trades has been much less harmful than might have been anticipated'. Unemployment in the city, it went on, was practically non-existent and if anything, Coventry was experiencing a shortage of labour.

M. J. DAVIES & SON,

General Drapers . .
Costumiers & Milliners,

BROADGATE, :: :: COVENTRY

View showing Dress and Blouse Showroom with a glimpse of Millinery Room above.

READY TO WEAR GOWNS FOR ALL OCCASIONS.

View showing DRESS and Silk Departments.

We specialise in Ladies' Motor Bonnets and Veils.

Davies & Son of Broadgate, one of Coventry's most prominent emporiums.

COURTESY OF DAVID FRY

In the first anxious weeks of the war, the Chamber itself, somewhat improbably, called for a revival of the city's old staple industries of watch-making and ribbon-making, both trades that had been almost obliterated half a century earlier by competition from the Continent and which more recently had been thriving in German hands.

Ancient watchmakers recalled that work had come back to the city during the Franco-Prussian war in 1870 and there were even hopes that a Coventry employer might be found to revive ribbon manufacturing. In the event, it was quickly realised that there was nobody left alive with the level of expertise needed to set up the industry and the idea was quietly dropped.

New Business

There was one vital sector of German trade, however, that the nation would have to replicate, and Coventry was quick to latch on to it. Before the war almost all the magnetos used in British engineering, notably in the ignition systems for motor vehicles, had been made in Germany, largely by Bosch in Stuttgart.

Britain would have to create a new magneto industry of its own. In November 1914 the Rugby-based electrical firm British Thomson Houston received its first order for 300 magnetos from the government, manufacturing them at the Alma Street factory it had established in the Hillfields district of Coventry in 1912.

By 1916, the Conner Magneto and Ignition Ltd, an offshoot of electrical giant GEC, had started its own production of magnetos in a new factory built on 10 acres of land acquired from the Copsewood estate in Stoke.

Another new development that autumn that had the Chamber very excited was the progress being made in sinking shafts for the new Coventry Colliery at Keresley, which would eventually go into full production in 1917.

The city, the Chamber argued, boasted the nearest coal field to London and in Keresley had a pit that was in the process of becoming the most important colliery in the country. It would, the Chamber predicted, be a great help to the city's prosperity.

War Footing

If coal was the fuel needed to power up Coventry's war effort, then its spark would be the speed with which the city's engineering industry could switch from peacetime production on to a war footing.

In the event, it appeared to be almost seamless. Before the end of the year twenty-five companies, more than ten per cent of the engineering sector in Coventry, were hard at work on the production of armaments. Machine tool firm Alfred Herbert was already sending capstan lathes to Britain's ally Russia, while engine manufacturer White and Poppe had taken its first order for fuse bodies for artillery shells before the end of August.

Nowhere was the call to arms more eagerly embraced than Coventry Ordnance Works (COW), under its energetic and innovative Managing Director, retired Rear-Admiral Reginald Bacon.

Set up in 1905 to break up the duopoly held by Armstrong and Vickers in Britain's heavy armaments industry, COW's fortunes had been decidedly mixed in the early years but had been transformed by the arrival of Bacon in 1910 and by the company's development of a 4.5-inch field howitzer, quickly adopted as the chief field weapon of the British and Canadian Armies.

Admiral Bacon, once described as the cleverest man in the Royal Navy, was a remote and forbidding figure. His instinctive grasp of engineering and Admiralty contacts meant that even before war broke out, the company was producing 100-ton naval guns for battleships at its 60-acre factory site off the Stoney Stanton Road.

COW had also experimented with aircraft production before the war, and as the munitions effort accelerated it received contracts from the Royal Aircraft Factory to make its B.E.2c aeroplane. The company would turn out more than 700 aircraft during the war, just one of a long list of products that would make COW one of the country's most important armaments manufacturers. Bacon later recalled that he spent almost all of his time in the winter of 1914 on the phone taking orders.

Alfred Herbert's machine shop, early in the war.

COURTESY OF MARK RADFORD

The vast interior of the Coventry Ordnance Works gun shop.

COURTESY OF THE
HERBERT HISTORY CENTRE

For the big names of Coventry industry, the war was clearly going to be a profitable enterprise and the more enlightened quickly realised that they had to go some way to support those they depended on – their workforce – many of whom had already patriotically answered the call to the colours.

A Caring Face

At the outbreak of war, the directors of the cycle and motorcycle manufacturer Rudge-Whitworth decided that for each former employee now in the service of the King they would pay 7s a week to wives and 1s a week for each child under the age of 14. Motorcycle manufacturer Triumph and the vehicle builder Maudslay established their own funds to support families while the men were away and many others quickly followed suit.

Rudge was among the leaders striving to make life a little more bearable for former employees at the front. At Christmas 1914 its gift parcel for soldiers included socks, mittens, body belts and woollen helmets, almost all knitted by female Rudge workers. Also enclosed was a company message from home, couched in slightly awkward verse:

It has filled our girls with pride and joy
To make these gifts for the soldier boys
If you thrive like a Rudge, and fear no (h)ill
I'm sure you will conquer Kaiser Bill.

While their menfolk practised their marching songs on the long straight roads of France, Coventry's war wives were adopting the name of a famous song for a new morale-booster of their own. In early 1915 the city's Women's Suffrage Society set up the Tipperary Club at Palace Yard in Earl Street to bring women relatives of serving men together 'to offer mutual assistance and comfort to each other'.

Apart from companionship, the club offered women facilities where they could read or write letters and established a nursery where their children could be looked after while they did so.

Under its progressive Medical Officer of Health, Dr Hugh Snell, Coventry had earned itself a forward-looking reputation for child welfare in the years before the war. As early as 1904,

Suffragettes had made their presence felt in Coventry in March 1914, pouring a 'noxious fluid' into post boxes at the city's main Post Office in Hertford Street, and later that month they had disrupted a Labour Party meeting at the Corn Exchange. But in a city where women increasingly found themselves part of the war effort, suffrage was not a burning issue.

A gathering of the Tipperary Club in Palace Yard.
COURTESY OF MARK RADFORD

local mothers were being issued with advice on breastfeeding and hygiene and within two years the city had its first health visitor, a Miss Strover. By 1914 there were three health vistors, ensuring that two-thirds of all women giving birth in Coventry received at least one visit from a health visitor each year.

The Triumph Company prepares Christmas parcels for its men on the front line.
COURTESY OF MARK RADFORD

Yet when, in October 1914, the government announced a new scheme to establish antenatal clinics in hospitals, with all children to be seen by health visitors, and furthermore offered local authorities a fifty per cent grant to help pay for it, the progressive in Dr Snell vanished.

There was no need for such a maternity centre in Coventry, he declared, because the city had, on account of its high wages and absence of poverty, the lowest death rate of any Midlands industrial city. True enough, but he omitted to mention the infant mortality rate in Coventry, which at ninety-two per thousand births still stood alarmingly high.

His intransigence united women from across the social spectrum in a defiant new Care of Maternity Committee, whose leading lights included both Mrs Frances Rotherham, wife of a prominent local employer, and Annie Corrie, a feisty member of the Women's Labour League.

Class strains were to later lead to divisions, in which the more middle-class Coventry Voluntary Infant Welfare Committee broke away and organised its own charitable clinic. But the tradition of a Saturday clinic being open to all, established by the Care of Maternity Committee at Palace Yard, persisted until 1917, when the city council was finally persuaded to take over the service and began operating it three afternoons a week.

The Face of War

Early in October, news came through of the first Coventry soldiers who had given their lives for King and Country. On 26 August, Private Nathaniel Hartley of 2nd Battalion, Lancashire Fusiliers was killed in action near Cambrai, aged 26. One day later, Private Tom Hazlewood of 1st Battalion, Gloucestershire Regiment was killed in the retreat from Mons.

Coventry lost another son on 18 September, when 29-year-old Private William Foster from the 1st Battalion, Royal Warwickshire Regiment died of wounds suffered in the Battle of the Aisne. An army reservist and tram conductor from the Little Heath

Coventry prisoners of war in Germany in 1915.

COURTESY OF MARK RADFORD

area of the city, he was well known in Coventry and his death was widely lamented.

The fast-moving battles of the first weeks of the war were also introducing the British public to a new phenomenon – the capture and imprisonment of their own men in large numbers. Among the first was Coventry soldier Private Alfred Charles Arkle, serving with the Yorkshire Light Infantry, who was captured by the Germans in August and sent to a prison camp at Dülmen in Westphalia, Western Germany.

Conditions at Dülmen were reasonable; throughout the war it was regarded as one of the better prisoner-of-war camps run by the Germans. But their record was not unblemished and in some camps disease and a deliberately brutal regime caused many deaths among prisoners. To public opinion back in Blighty this would come to exemplify the barbarism of the Kaiser's cause.

It's not possible to calculate accurately how many men Coventry sent to the war. The figure of 35,000, used in more modern times, seems exaggerated. A more likely figure is around 25,000.

Those who felt like that from the outset could also point to German attacks on Britain to bolster their argument. On 16 December 1914 cruisers from the German High Seas fleet bombarded the defenceless towns of Scarborough, Whitby and Hartlepool, killing more than a hundred men, women and children.

Threat from the Air

Public outrage at attacks from the sea on helpless civilians was compounded early in January by something even more heinous: an attack from the air by a German airship on the Norfolk town of Great Yarmouth, in which two people were killed.

In Coventry, the first lethal raid by a Zeppelin raised many troubling questions. Great Yarmouth was 85 miles away and it had always been assumed that Coventry lay outside the enemy range. But was that really true? If not, would Coventry and its accelerating munitions industry be an early target?

Painting out the skylights in the Corn Exchange roof.

COURTESY OF MARK RADFORD

Particular concern centred on the huge Coventry Ordnance Works, which many people believed would be familiar to German military planners as the German industrial giant Krupps had helped to build it in 1905.

The decision was taken to prepare the city for the very real possibility of air raids and in early February Coventry's Chief Constable Charles Charsley reported that an application had been made under the Defence of the Realm Act for the reduction or extinction of building and street lights in the city, in line with similar action taken in Birmingham. At the same time, further action was taken to prevent light flooding into the sky by painting over 'culprits' like the skylights in the roof of the city's Corn Exchange.

As a government propaganda campaign was launched, Coventrians were issued with instructions for the event of an air-raid warning. 'No need for undue alarm,' they began. 'Avoid the streets as you could be an impediment to the authorities. Take shelter in the basements of buildings and be aware that it may be found necessary to plunge the city into darkness.'

The aim of the lighting restrictions, which came into force on 12 April, was to take out some street lamps, breaking up the long lines of lights as seen from the air, with what remained being shaded from above. Other restrictions controlled lighting in shops, factories and places of entertainment and there were penalties for breaches of the regulations – up to six months in prison or a fine of up to £100.

Among the first to feel the weight of this new law was Sarah Luckman, the proprietor of a music shop in Hertford Street, who in May was fined £2 for refusing to effectively shade and obscure her shop windows.

Not everybody was sanguine about the cut in lighting. Some viewed it as a danger to life and limb and the Revd P.E.T. Widdrington, vicar of St Peter's church in Hillfields, was concerned that women munitions workers would be at risk if they had to use darkened alleyways in the area to get to their work.

Comfort in the Home.

THE idea in the mind of every Mistress of the Home when considering Furnishings and Decorations is to combine comfort with beauty, and also to satisfy her individual taste.

Customers will tell you that Anslow's is a Furnishing House where the virtues of **QUALITY** and **ECONOMY** are combined. If you have not received

A Copy of the Catalogue

" Comfort in the Home " please call or write for one : you will find therein many delightful suggestions for Furnishing which will please you. If you cannot call, a copy will be sent post free upon application.

JOHN ANSLOW LIMITED.
HIGH STREET & HAY LANE. COVENTRY.   II.P.

Soft furnishers like Anslow's could supply a better class of blackout curtain.

COURTESY OF MARK RADFORD

At an inquest into the death of an elderly gardener named Dodds, who died after his bicycle collided with a man and a woman in the dark, Coventry's coroner concluded that the couple must have been German as they had run off after the accident.

Defending the Realm

By early October 1914 in Coventry, it was unlawful to own a homing pigeon without a special permit and anybody caught shooting one could receive a sentence of six months in prison. Homing pigeons, the public were reminded, were doing valuable work for the government and there was a £5 reward for information leading to a conviction.

The special status given to a bird that in some quarters might be regarded as vermin was one consequence of the Defence of the Realm Act (DORA). This was rushed through Parliament four days after the outbreak of war to give government the power to requisition land or buildings for the war effort and to draft in a whole new flotilla of criminal offences for actions deemed to be giving aid to the enemy.

'No person,' the legislation stated, 'shall by word of mouth or in writing spread reports likely to cause dissatisfaction or alarm among His Majesty's forces or the civil population.'

While that clearly meant strictures against discussing naval or military matters in public, the Act also outlawed flying kites, starting bonfires, buying binoculars, feeding bread to wild animals or buying alcohol on public transport.

In London, it was an offence to whistle for a taxi, in case it might be mistaken for an air-raid warning. Loitering near tunnels or bridges was a criminal offence, as was using white flour instead of wholemeal in baking. Possession of cocaine and heroin was criminalised too.

The Act introduced British Summer Time, to maximise hours in the working day. It restricted pub opening hours to 12 p.m. to 3 p.m. and 6.30 p.m. to 9.30 p.m., leaving a compulsory gap in the drinking day that lasted until 1988. It watered down the beer and made it an offence to buy a round of drinks in a pub.

And if anybody felt that these were trivial measures, then breaching DORA with intent could be lethal. In the course of the war ten people were executed in Britain for breaching regulations to aid the enemy.

The Act also allowed the Admiralty and the Army Council to take control of any workshop or factory, for their own purposes; a provision very much of interest to Coventry.

A Friendly Billet

As Coventry's young men enlisted and marched away to war, the city acquired a whole new army of sons to look after as they prepared to put their lives on the line for King and Country.

Within four days in January 1915 more than 2,000 soldiers arrived in Coventry en route for the battlefields. The first to arrive were 236 men, ten officers and thirty horses from the 88th (1st East Anglian) Field Ambulance, a Territorial unit of the Royal Army Medical Corps. They were followed in quick order by the 1st Battalion, the Royal Munster Fusiliers (twenty-one officers, 875 men) and the 2nd Battalion South Wales Borderers (twenty-two officers, 892 men).

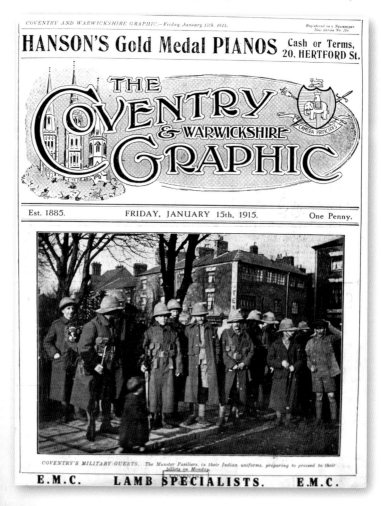

COVENTRY AND WARWICKSHIRE GRAPHIC.—Friday, January 15th, 1915.

Registered as a Newspaper.
New Series No. 170.

HANSON'S Gold Medal PIANOS Cash or Terms, 20, HERTFORD St.

THE COVENTRY & WARWICKSHIRE GRAPHIC

Est. 1885. FRIDAY, JANUARY 15th, 1915. One Penny.

COVENTRY'S MILITARY GUESTS. *The Munster Fusiliers, in their Indian uniforms, preparing to proceed to their billets on Monday.*

E.M.C. **LAMB SPECIALISTS.** E.M.C.

Front page news. Munster Fusiliers preparing for their billets.

COURTESY OF MARK RADFORD

The marriage of Lieutenant Tim Sullivan and Maud Bates.
COURTESY OF MARK RADFORD

Unusually, they were not garrisoned in military establishments like Coventry Barracks, but were billeted with local families, an age-old tradition that had fallen out of favour with the British Army in the middle of the nineteenth century.

Initially there were fears that billeting would expose young Coventry women to licentious soldiery, yet it was to prove highly successful. For a start, it was calculated that the soldiers' presence ensured that an extra £2,000 a week was being pumped into the city's economy. But the bonds between them and their hosts went a lot deeper than that, especially in the case of the Munster Fusiliers, who were billeted largely in Earlsdon.

Despite the hardships of their first few days in Coventry – they arrived in bleak January weather wearing the tropical kit of pith helmets and shorts from their previous posting in Burma – the geniality and good humour of these Irishmen won the hearts of Coventry folk, and fond memories of them lingered long after.

For some, friendship burgeoned into deeper feelings. Lieutenant Tim Sullivan, recently commissioned from the ranks, became the first Munster Fusilier to take a local wife when he married Miss Maud Bates from the family who owned the Albany Hotel in Earlsdon, at St Osburg's church on 4 March.

When they departed for the Gallipoli campaign a few days later, the Munsters were given a scroll of thanks on behalf of the people of Coventry, dedicated to 'our soldiers'. It was a genuine expression of fondness that irritated many serving Coventry soldiers, who peppered city newspapers with letters from the

Munster Fusilier Buller – mascot and survivor.

front line in France questioning why they too had not been given such a memento from their own city.

The Munsters left Coventry with another gift, an 18-month-old English bull terrier named Buller, presented to them by Billy Williamson, a local industrialist. The gift came complete with a special coat for the dog, with the arms of Coventry on one side and an emerald green regimental badge on the other, plus a stipend of 8s 9d a week, half the rate that a family would get for each soldier billeted to them.

Buller, who had been billeted at the City Arms in Earlsdon, landed with the rest of the battalion at the infamous V Beach at Cape Helles on 26 April and survived the inferno that awaited them, being taken off the beach and evacuated by ship some time later.

His human comrades were less fortunate. The Munsters were shattered in the landing and the bloody and ultimately futile campaign that followed, with almost 600 men killed, wounded or taken prisoner. Among the dead was the newly married Lieutenant Sullivan, who died of his wounds on 4 May, leaving poor Maud a widow. In Coventry, the losses were deeply felt.

3

WORK OF WAR

In the first week of January 1915, police swooped on a house in Foleshill Road, Coventry and arrested Arthur Johnson, a blacksmith working at the Coventry Ordnance Works (COW), on suspicion of spying.

Johnson had been employed by the company in November after spending the previous twelve months working at the site of the proposed Coventry Colliery in Keresley. After a series of vague and unsubstantiated spy scares in the early months of the war, it looked as though the police had finally nabbed a bona fide secret agent.

His real name turned out to be Arthur Prozky. He was a gun engineer by profession and his true employers, it was said, were the German Naval Department. He claimed to be an American, born in Boston, but he spoke with a strong German accent and he had told a curious landlady in Cardiff, where he'd worked before the war, that he actually hailed from Danzig.

Prozky may well have been the genuine article but, surprisingly, was not charged with being a spy. Instead, he was convicted of failing to register with the city magistrates as an enemy alien and was sentenced to three months' hard labour.

The case highlighted a potential threat to COW, at the time undoubtedly the city's biggest contributor to the nation's munitions needs, and steps were hurriedly taken to beef up security. A detachment of fourteen soldiers from the Duke of Cornwall's Light

It is estimated that around 60,000 people were engaged in war work in Coventry during the Great War, up to half of them brought into the city each day from surrounding areas and as far away as Birmingham.

Soldiers and cannon guard the Ordnance works.

COURTESY OF MARK RADFORD

Infantry was deployed to guard the factory gates, armed with a small cannon, pointed skywards, while the city's air-raid defences were strengthened with new anti-aircraft gun emplacements at Keresley, Wyken Croft and Pinley.

The Ordnance Works would go on to have a very productive war, turning out more than 700 aircraft, hundreds of thousands of shell casings, guns and armour for some of the biggest ships in Britain's mighty navy, siege howitzers and field guns for the army, and in 1917 a 37mm gun that was the world's first automatic cannon.

But it was the secret work it carried out for the War Department on a potentially war-winning new weapon that would have made it an especially tempting target for espionage.

The Moving Fort

The journalist Henry Wilkins picked up word of this work in early January 1915 and recorded it in his *Journal of the European War*:

> I hear of the Ordnance Works and Daimler staff evolving a motor machine able to run over military trenches. It is to be of armoured steel, large enough to contain many soldiers, who could fire from their moving fort and the machine being covered would be free from assault, except from artillery fire.

The tank would go on to prove itself a decisive weapon in the eventual Allied victory. It has never been strongly associated with Coventry, yet from those first 'evolutions' it is clear that the city's armaments manufacturers played a key role in its creation and development.

COW's forceful and innovative managing director, Admiral Reginald Bacon, soon to be recalled to active service as Commanding Officer of the Dover Patrol, was a key player in this. At its 60-acre Coventry site, COW produced armour plating for the new 'moving fort' and later on built more than a hundred tanks in its own right at its factory in Glasgow. Daimler, the other partner in those early 'evolutions', produced the engines for this new weapon. The Rover Company supplied transmission systems, while Coventry Chain made the tracks.

Significantly too, there were many Coventry men among the early tank crews, their engineering skills and instinctive understanding of vehicle mechanics making them fitting handlers of a machine that would revolutionise the battlefield.

Among the first was Gunner Walter Atkins from Bell Green, who was called up in February 1916, enlisted in the Machine Gun Corps and then joined one of the first tank crews. One of the first to drive a tank in combat, he went into action at Martinpuich on the Somme on 15 September 1916 in tank D20, nicknamed Daphne, serving alongside a kitten named Percy who was a good luck mascot of the tank commander, Lieutenant Harry Drader.

Atkins received a gunshot wound in the shoulder during the Somme campaign and was evacuated back to England, where he recovered from his injuries in hospital in Manchester. Sent to Bovington Camp in Dorset to prepare for his return to France, he was taken seriously ill with appendicitis in February 1917 and sadly died on the operating table through 'incorrect administration of chloroform'.

Unrivalled Record

Coventry's work on the evolution of the tank, it was later claimed, was arguably the city's most important single contribution to the war effort, but the scale and range of that contribution was truly staggering.

More than 200 companies played their part, turning out a bewildering range of products, from tiny jewels used in precision instruments to 100-ton naval guns, from the chains used on aeroplane cameras to field kitchens, and from seaplane chassis to chronometers for the Royal Navy.

Coventry produced a quarter of all the aircraft made in Britain during the war and made more aero engines than anywhere else. Many companies added munitions to their other products, turning out shell cases, fuses and detonators by the tens and hundreds of thousands.

By early 1915 the government was taking a firm grip on all these activities. Two of the biggest players, COW and Alfred Herbert, became the first companies in Coventry to be 'controlled' by the War Department, barred from accepting any work from other clients. Before the end of the year nearly fifty Coventry firms were on the 'controlled' list.

For the smaller companies, a new body, the Coventry Armaments Output Committee, was set up to help them in their dealings with the government. It was run by Alfred Bednell, who had been a cycle manufacturer in Coventry as far back as the late 1880s and had wide contacts and a broad understanding of the city's engineering sector.

Maudslay lorries ready for action at the front.
COURTESY OF MARK RADFORD

He used the Coventry and Country Club, established back in 1889 as an informal watering hole for the city's industrialists, as a base for the new committee and would operate from its bar, where most of his business was done.

The Shell Crisis

In March 1915, the British launched their first serious attempt to break out of the growing stalemate of trench warfare in an offensive that became known as the Battle of Neuve Chapelle, three days of intense fighting in which both sides suffered horrific casualties.

At first the British made major advances, but the attack was slowed by communications problems and delays, allowing the Germans to regroup and push the advance back almost to its starting point.

A critical factor was a crippling shortage of ammunition for artillery. It was estimated that the British Army needed around 480,000 high-explosive shells to press home its advantage, but only had 52,000 at its disposal.

As a consequence, the national newspapers at home went on the warpath; Asquith's Liberal government fell, to be replaced by a coalition; and the astute and dynamic David Lloyd George became the new Minister of Munitions.

Lloyd George's first move was to come to an agreement with the trade unions, notably the Amalgamated Society of Engineers, that would stop the most highly skilled men from being allowed to join the army and would introduce 'dilution', by which companies could begin to take on more unskilled labour, including women, to boost production. He also proposed a national network of new factories to manufacture shells and fuses.

All of this had a major impact on Coventry. Women began to play a serious role in the conduct of the war locally and White and Poppe Ltd, an engine manufacturer that had already turned itself into a maker of munitions, was allowed to develop the huge National Shell-filling Factory No. 10 on green fields near its sprawling works in Holbrooks.

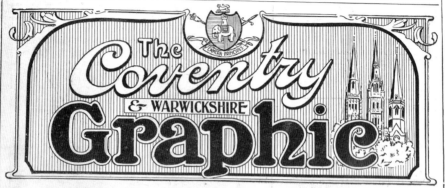

COVENTRY AND WARWICKSHIRE GRAPHIC.—Friday, March 3rd, 1916.

Registered as a Newspaper.
New Series No. 249.

E. J. GODFREY,   LADIES' TAILOR.   ONLY ADDRESS—
218, FOLESHILL ROAD.

The Coventry & Warwickshire Graphic

LARGEST CIRCULATION OF ANY WEEKLY PAPER IN COVENTRY.

Est. 1885.   FRIDAY, MARCH 3rd, 1916.   One Penny.

A Corner of the Shell Department at the Standard Motor Works.   *Other pictures appear overleaf.*

E.M.C.   PRIME OX BEEF.   COVENTRY CITY LIBRARIES   E.M.C.

Making shells at Standard.

COURTESY OF MARK RADFORD

The boost this gave to the city as a core contributor to the war effort was highlighted in a dispute about power generation. Coventry desperately needed more electricity to supply its new factories, and placed an order with the British Thomson Houston Company for a 3,000kW turbo alternator. The order was initially held up as Chatham Dockyard in Kent was regarded as having priority, but a high-powered delegation to the Admiralty from some of Coventry's biggest companies, including the Ordnance and White and Poppe, swiftly managed to overturn that decision.

> Government spending on armaments and munitions with Coventry manufacturers during the war amounted to £40.5 million, the equivalent of £2.5 billion today.

The importance and performance of the city as a munitions centre later led o some of its major industrial figures being given supervisory roles in government ministries. Percy Martin (Daimler's highly respected American general manager), Admiral Bacon and the printer and newspaper owner Edward Iliffe were all recruited into the Ministry to supervise different areas of production.

But the most important task went to machine tool manufacturer Alfred Herbert, who was called in to help supervise his own industry in the spring of 1915 and two years later was appointed Controller of the Machine Tool section of the Ministry. Herbert's firm was already the biggest in Britain and he'd been President of the Machine Tools Trades Association for many years before the war, but his new role at the heart of government contracts was controversial.

After introducing price restrictions for firms in the industry, Herbert was subjected to a campaign of vilification from rivals, hitting at him through *The Globe* newspaper, which at one point threatened to run a story accusing him of conspiring with American investors to secure a monopoly of the machine tool industry after the war.

Herbert was unmoved. 'When I undertook control of the machine tool industry,' he wrote later, 'I knew that I should have to face much criticism and suspicion. It was part of my contract to be prepared for this and I was not dismayed by it.'

The knighthood he received for his work in 1917 must have further infuriated his enemies, but there is no evidence that he unfairly favoured his own company at the expense of competitors.

A Munitions Giant

In 1897, Alfred White, son of a Coventry watch-maker, and Peter Poppe, a Norwegian engineer, decided to set up in business together making engines.

By the summer of 1914, with a workforce of 350, they had supplied forty-eight different manufacturers with engines for automobiles, locomotives, boats and aeroplanes from their factory in Drake Street, Foleshill.

Yet within two years White and Poppe had turned itself into one of the country's biggest munitions firms, manufacturing shell fuses and detonators by the million in a giant factory complex that stretched over 140 acres and was serviced by 6½ miles of railway sidings.

By June 1915 the company had taken on its first thirty women workers and was just completing a new factory on what had been cornfields along rural Holbrook Lane, supported by a government grant of £813,400. By the end of 1916 it employed 4,000 women and 800 men in its new National Filling Factory No. 10 (later changed to No. 21 after a quality control problem with shells from some of its suppliers made front-line artillerymen wary of using its products).

It had become a small town, with a forty-bed hospital and a police force of thirty-five. It had almost 100 acres of ground under cultivation for food. It had a swimming pool, library, cinema and a canteen that could serve 36,000 meals in a twenty-four-hour period.

The production figures are impressive. By the end of the war White and Poppe had turned out 20 million fuses and 31 million detonators. Its railway sidings had dealt with 50,000 trains, bringing in raw materials each night and taking away finished products – 322,000 tons of them.

But it was as an employer of female munitions workers, dubbed Canary Girls because the toxic materials they were handling turned their skin yellow, that the company was most notable.

They wore blue uniforms, with a coloured armband on the right sleeve to denote where they came from – red for England, green for Ireland, blue for Scotland and pale blue for Wales. Hostels and cottages built by the company on site could house 5,700 female workers at any one time and by the end of the war it was estimated that 24,000 women had 'done their bit' with White and Poppe.

White and Poppe workers at home in Holbrooks.

A Woman's War?

There was one aspect of Coventry's war work to which Alfred Herbert was to prove something of a convert – the employment of women.

Reluctant at first – he felt 'fundamental differences in mentality' meant that women in general could not become skilled mechanics – he accepted they had a role to play and became an influential voice urging others with similar prejudices to follow suit.

There were plenty of those. In the years before the First World War, employers and trade unions like the Amalgamated Society of Engineers had made it very difficult for women to work in anything except the clerical side of engineering companies. In 1906, the Triumph Company had boasted in its recruitment advertising that it was the only bicycle company in Coventry *not* to employ women.

All that began to change in the spring and early summer of 1915. In June, women in uniform began to appear on Coventry trams as conductors. They were spotted at the railway station, working as ticket collectors, and even began delivering the post, reduced during wartime to just three deliveries a day. Within months they were actually driving trams.

Women tram conductors in 1915.

COURTESY OF MARK RADFORD

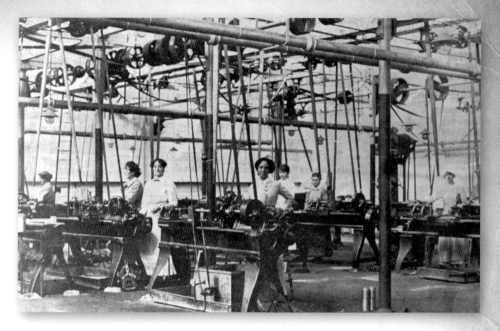

*Women munitions
workers at the
Hillman factory.*
COURTESY OF MARK RADFORD

The first industrialist to openly advocate the employment of
women in war work was cycle and automobile manufacturer
William Hillman, who, by August, had set up his own modest shell
factory in Lower Ford Street, employing several hundred women.
'If anyone else is prepared to follow my example,' he wrote, 'I am
prepared to show him that women can make these things and
make them properly. He can come and see every operation in
making the shell, from the beginning to the end.'

The rapid explosion in the numbers of female munitions
workers, in particular, put huge strains on the already crippling
shortage of living accommodation in Coventry. As thousands
poured in from all corners of the British Isles, it was immediately
obvious that the city could simply not house them all. Sharing
a single bed on a shift rota basis, as happened to many, would
simply not suffice. Before long, up to 16,000 munitions workers,
the majority of them women, had sought accommodation in
neighbouring towns and villages and were being brought into
Coventry every day by bus, train and tram.

Gertrude Sellors arrived from Yorkshire with her husband to
work at White and Poppe, testing fuses, and as a married couple
they managed to find a house to rent not far from the works.

Gertrude became a supervisor, looking after a corridor of female munitions workers, and she recalled the vast scale of the complex, with the facilities of a small town and an entertainment programme that included Gilbert and Sullivan operas, staged by actors from London theatres which had been closed down due to the war.

But she remembered too the risks the women ran working with cordite, which could induce fits; TNT, which caused toxic jaundice, turning the skin yellow and the hair green; and Composition Exploding or tetryl, which caused the skin of its victims to turn yellow, giving rise to the nickname of these courageous munitions workers as Canary Girls.

Through careful management and with a large dose of luck thrown in, White and Poppe did not suffer the sort of cataclysmic accident that happened at another of the national shell factories at Chilwell in Nottinghamshire. A factory explosion there in the spring of 1918 killed 139 workers, most of them women.

But there were many minor accidents and major alarms were not uncommon. It wasn't unknown for local residents to have to intercept and calm down workers as they fled through surrounding streets.

Coventry Canary Girl Mabel Ford recalled the day that one of the detonator sheds blew up. 'I remember girls fainting and screaming. There was great panic and some were found as far away as the city centre, still in their caps and gowns.'

Munitions workers at Foleshill Station. Thousands travelled into the city each day.

COURTESY OF
MARK RADFORD

White and Poppe Canary Girls.

Officially, there was just one fatality. On 23 July 1917, Ada Curtis, working in one of the high-risk fulminate shops, died from the injuries she received when she dropped a detonator she was carrying.

The exposure to such risks meant that by the standards of the day the women doing this dangerous work were highly paid. Foleshill resident Elsie Bentley recalled many years later that a 16-year-old Welsh girl billeted with her family was earning almost £3 a week, a significant wage for a skilled worker.

By November 1916, one Coventry bank manager estimated that £130,000 was being paid out in wages in the city every week. Over the course of the war Coventrians also put in more than four million hours of unpaid voluntary work.

As Gertrude Sellors remembered, high wages were another source of resentment among those who did not like the idea of women doing a man's job. There were claims in the press that girls were being paid more than they knew what to do with and were frittering money away on fancy goods like fur coats, items that were well out of their league.

Others feared that women, while doing a good job, were damaging themselves by working in such inhospitable and dangerous places, a view that gained ground when it was revealed in early 1916 that a small number of women were being employed at Exhall and Newdigate collieries, picking shale from coal on the pit banks.

By that time, companies like White and Poppe were putting in place special facilities for the health and well-being of their female workforce, while the first city-wide social centre for young women moving into Coventry to work had been opened at a house called Brooklyn on the Foleshill Road as early as May 1915.

Nevertheless, the working lives of those women were being strictly controlled. The Munitions of War Act, given Royal Assent in July 1915, regulated wages and conditions and among many other provisions made it a penal offence for a munitions worker to leave a company 'controlled' by the government without special consent. Disputes over this highly restrictive regulation, which applied to both men and women, would come to dog labour relations in Coventry later in the war.

A Good War?

Coventry's importance as a munitions centre led to a morale-boosting royal visit to the city, the first of the war. King George V spent a day in Coventry in late July 1915, touring some of the city's big industrial players during an unpublicised visit that the censors insisted should be kept out of the local newspapers, much to their irritation.

The King went first to COW, then on to Daimler and Alfred Herbert, before ending up in the showrooms of the Rover Company in Warwick Row, where he was photographed

George V inspecting munitions at Rover.
COURTESY OF MARK RADFORD

inspecting a range of products representative of the city's rapidly growing contribution.

His visit coincided with a new push to recruit more skilled munitions workers to feed Coventry's expanding engineering companies, with St Mary's Hall acting as the headquarters for a Munitions Work Bureau that by August had recruited almost 1,900, mainly older, men.

After the spring Shell Crisis on the Western Front, the need to retain more skilled labour had become pressing. But there were those who had spotted that requirement some time before. Back in November 1914, Admiral Bacon, Coventry Ordnance Works' managing director, had taken it upon himself to write a personal letter to each of his 4,000-strong workforce. In it he wrote:

> My attention has been called to the fact that many men belonging to the Coventry Ordnance Works have been approached by well-meaning but misguided people in Coventry who exert pressure on them to enlist in some branch of HM forces.
>
> Such action is in absolute opposition to the wishes of Lord Kitchener and I would draw your attention to his letter of September 8 in which he impresses on you that you are serving your country far better by using your special skill in the supply of armaments required in the present war than by joining the colours.

If therefore at any time you are approached with a view to enlistment it would be advisable to show this letter in order to point out that if you left your urgent work for service in the field, you would be acting contrary to the best interests of your country.

THE COVENTRY ORDNANCE WORKS LIMITED.

ORDNANCE WORKS,

COVENTRY.

November 17th 1914

Dear Sir,

My attention has been called to the fact that many men belonging to the Coventry Ordnance Works have been approached by well meaning but mis-guided people in Coventry who exert pressure on them to enlist in some branch of H.M. Forces.

Such action is in absolute opposition to the wishes of Lord Kitchener —

In support of this I would draw your attention to Lord Kitcheners letter dated September 8th in which he impresses on you that you are serving your country far better by using your special skill in the supply of armaments required in the present war than by joining the colours. Lord Kitchener has also informed me that he will, as far as he possibly can, arrange for the return of men to these works who have enlisted.

The reason for Lord Kitcheners desire is obvious — An army without armaments is useless!

Part of Admiral Bacon's letter.

Shrewdly, Bacon went on to praise the efforts COW workers were making to complete the munitions required 'so as to bring this stupendous war to an early and successful close'.

Nationally, Coventry's achievements as a munitions power-house were acknowledged by *The Times* newspaper in January 1916. 'One finds in Coventry,' it declared, 'a note of industrial pride, perhaps more evident than anywhere else in the country. Local people believe the city has set a pace unequalled in the West.'

An American journalist, quoted in the article, went even further. 'The people of Coventry walk quicker than other Englishmen,' he wrote. 'There is a briskness in the very air of the place. Everyone seems prosperous. Everyone seems busy. Your factories are growing as fast as the factories in Detroit and I can't say more than that.'

He was almost certainly referring to a new factory being built in the city for the French Hotchkiss company, which had been chased out of Paris by the German advance in late 1914 and now, a year later, was on its way to becoming the British Army's main supplier of machine guns.

In November 1915, medieval houses in Gosford Street had been unceremoniously swept away, to the anguish of the city's new Civic Guild, and in just seven weeks the new five-storey Hotchkiss factory had been erected on the site and was almost ready to start production. In most places, *The Times* noted admiringly, plans would barely have been drawn up in that time.

By early 1916, Coventry's City Engineer was reporting that forty-six new factories had been completed in the year just past, and the pace of building had not slowed down.

It was a standing joke among the workforce of Rudge-Whitworth that under cover of darkness every night the company added another storey to its huge Spon Street factory to secure more production space. The Standard Company, hitherto not one of Coventry's largest players in the field of armaments, completed work in the autumn of 1916 on a new factory at Canley that would help it to become the biggest manufacturer of flying machines in the city, producing more than 1,500 aircraft in just two years.

The Triumph Company, run by the 'enemy alien' Siegfried Bettmann, made more than 30,000 of its Model 'H' motorcycles for the British Army during the war. The workforce at Siddeley-Deasy, another of Coventry's medium-scale engineering companies, grew from 400 in August 1914 to more than 6,000 at the end of the war, largely because of its work in aviation, notably the production of 11,500 Puma aero engines.

The Hotchkiss factory, rising in just seven weeks.
COURTESY OF THE
HERBERT HISTORY CENTRE

Aero engine strippers at Siddeley-Deasy, later in the war.
COURTESY OF DAVID FRY

Individual Talent

But amidst all this frenzy of factory-building and workforce expansion among companies there was still room for the talented individual.

Before the war, John Frank Buckingham had been a small-time manufacturer of light cars at his modest premises in Spon Street. With the market for light cars dead on its feet, the inventive Mr Buckingham swiftly turned his attention to developing an incendiary bullet that could threaten the dreaded Zeppelins.

Buckingham took out his first patent for a tracer bullet, based on phosphorous, in January 1915. Trial bullets were sent to the Ministry of War in October and they went into service with the Royal Naval Air Service before the end of the year.

The firm went on to make a staggering twenty-six million Buckingham Bullets and it was later claimed that they had accounted for all but one of the Zeppelins shot down over England during the war.

Coventry's growing reputation for innovation led the Ministry to point in its direction other talented engineers with ideas in need of realisation.

Car company founder Walter Owen Bentley was sent to the city to work with Humber, and later Daimler, on developing a new aero engine that he had invented. Bentley's highly effective rotary engines were later fitted to the Sopwith Camel, Britain's foremost fighter aircraft, which was credited with winning back air superiority from the Germans and shooting down 1,294 enemy aircraft, more than any other British plane.

The furious pace and scale of Coventry's war work never failed to astonish outsiders. On a visit to Daimler in 1916, a journalist from the *London Evening Standard* wrote:

Children were encouraged to make sacrifices for the war effort.

COURTESY OF DAVID FRY

THE GREAT WAR,
1914, 1915.

This is to bear witness that the holder *Horace Wright*, with all the other Scholars of the Stoke Church Sunday School, went without a Summer Treat in the Year 1915, in order to help in the War by giving the money saved from the Treat to the Red Cross Fund.

A.R.F. Hyslop. Rector.

J.S. Webb }

Ethel M. Clarke } Superintendents.

STOKE, COVENTRY, AUGUST, 1915.

The whole place hums with activity. As I went through great sheds
where men were fitting up motor ambulances, and machine shops
where engines for both motors and aeroplanes were being made
and other shops where shells were being manufactured, and when
I stood out on the flying field where aeroplanes were being tested,
I felt that here was the finest repudiation of the story that one
sometimes hears that England is not doing her share.

In the city itself, the impulse to be seen 'doing your bit' extended even
to the boys of Bablake School, who in the summer of 1916 were
offered the opportunity of spending at least some of their summer
holidays working at White and Poppe. Some eighty boys signed up
and while it is not absolutely clear what they were being asked to do
in such a dangerous working environment, the school itself was fully
behind them. 'We cannot imagine a more interesting or profitable
way of spending one's vacation,' commented the school magazine.

But not all rejoiced in that kind of patriotic fervour. Many
expressed doubts about the impact that munitions fever was having
on the people of the city.

In the summer of 1915, George Arbuthnot, Archdeacon of
Coventry, preached a sermon at St Michael's church in which he
warned of those effects. 'Fortunes are being made in Coventry
but the people are profiting little. There's a sad indifference on the
part of the rich to the conditions of the working classes.'

As pressures on working people increased – the average daily
shift at the Ordnance, for example, began at 6 a.m. and often did
not end until 8 p.m. – there was bound to be an explosion. And
it wasn't long in coming.

4

NEWS FROM THE FRONT

At Sea

Writing in *The Coventrian*, the school magazine of King Henry VIII School in Coventry, former pupil Edward Leslie Peirson described his first experience of battle. 'I think we took a good toll of the Huns,' wrote Peirson, then serving as a gunnery range-finder aboard the battleship HMS *Vanguard*. 'We were able to hit an enemy cruiser and there is little doubt that she went down. We were in action about two hours and I'm unable to say if we actually damaged any other ships, but I'm sure that when the time comes, this ship, for one, will not fail to give a good account of herself.'

Peirson, the son of a well-known Coventry chartered accountant, was writing about the Battle of Jutland on 31 May 1916, the most important naval encounter of the war between the navies of Britain and Germany.

It was a battle that took the lives of at least six Coventry sailors, among them Charles John Jones, a gunnery Warrant Officer serving aboard HMS *Queen Mary*; Henry Gordon Farmer, aged just 16, a Boy 1st Class, killed by a shell on board HMS *Malaya*; and another Boy 1st Class, Horace Blunt, also 16 and a former telegraph boy at Coventry Railway Station, killed aboard HMS *Defence*.

But if Peirson saw Jutland as a thrilling introduction to naval warfare, then his conclusion would be tragically soon. Little more than a year later, shortly before midnight on 9 July 1917, he was one of more than 800 men lost when HMS *Vanguard* suddenly blew up at anchor in Scapa Flow, the biggest loss of life in an accidental explosion in British history. He was just 26.

In the aftermath of the accident there was initially talk of sabotage and bizarrely, Peirson, who had been the ship's Assistant Paymaster, was the chief suspect. His name, it was said, was spelled the German way, he'd studied accountancy at Heidelberg University before the war and a letter written in German had been found among his possessions. He'd also declined to join brother officers that evening at a concert aboard another ship.

Thankfully, these ludicrous calumnies were quickly shown to be false and he was given a proper funeral service and memorial stone at Coventry's London Road cemetery.

None of Coventry's small band of seafarers could boast a wartime record quite as lurid as solicitor's son Godfrey Herbert, another former pupil of King Henry VIII School and a career naval officer since 1898.

When war broke out, Herbert was commanding Submarine D5, in which he tried to torpedo but missed the German cruiser SMS *Rostock*, a failure that a later Board of Enquiry attributed partly to bad luck and partly to incompetence. Herbert went on to survive not one but two submarine sinkings and to invent a torpedo that could be 'ridden' by one man, an idea turned down flat by Admiralty chiefs but finally turned into reality during the Second World War.

But it was as skipper of the 'Q' ship HMS *Baralong*, an armed warship disguised as a merchantman, that Herbert committed what in a different age might be considered a war crime.

Called to the aid of a merchant ship that was being boarded by sailors from a German submarine, U-27, Herbert unfurled the White Ensign as he approached, sank the U-boat, machine-gunned its crew in the water and then sent in Royal Marines to finish off any German sailors surviving aboard the merchant ship.

His brutal actions prompted outrage from the ship's American passengers and the German Government, but it turned out that Herbert was acting on Admiralty orders not to take prisoners from German submarines. The order

Among those lost alongside Lord Kitchener when the cruiser HMS *Hampshire* was sunk by a German mine on its way to Russia in June 1916 was David Cliffe Brown from Coventry, a driver with the Royal Field Artillery.

had gone out in the aftermath of the sinking of the Cunard ocean liner RMS *Lusitania* off the coast of Ireland on 7 May 1915, with the loss of almost 1,200 lives. And it reflected the widely held view that there was something devilish about submarine warfare and that U-boat crews were pirates and deserved nothing less than a merciless end.

The *Lusitania* tragedy itself had been keenly felt in Coventry. Among those lost was Scottish-born Walter Wright, manager of the wheel department at the city's Dunlop Rim and Wheel Company, who lived in the upmarket Stoke Park estate. Wright had been on business in America and had telegraphed his wife to say that he was returning on the *Lusitania*. He was never heard from again and his body was never found, but like Peirson he was given a memorial service and a headstone at London Road cemetery.

Walter Wright, pictured on his fateful business trip to America.

COURTESY OF THE WRIGHT FAMILY

On Land

By August 1915 the army's pressing need for new recruits had turned the 7th Royal Warwickshire Regiment, the Territorial battalion raised in Coventry, into three service battalions.

The 1/7 had marched away to training at the outbreak of war and had landed in France in March 1915. The 2/7, raised over that first winter, was about to go, while the 3/7 was in training and would leave Coventry for service, largely spent in reserve in the UK, in mid-January 1916.

That same month another unit, almost entirely comprised of Coventry engineers, embarked for France to do its bit. The Coventry Fortress Company, raised in the city with the Mayor acting as recruiting sergeant, became 214 Army Troops Company, Royal Engineers and was to have an eventful war, operating just behind the lines in a variety of engineering and support roles.

First employed to cut down trees and run sawmills, the company was then thrown into action as emergency stretcher-bearers during the Battle of the Somme. Later it was sent to Ypres, where it carried out road repairs and construction, and then on to Arras, where it prepared the second line of defence. Finally, it was building bridges in Belgium when the Armistice was declared.

As the Fortress Company was beginning its foreign service, fears were being expressed in local newspapers that Coventry was not pulling its weight when it came to recruitment. By January 1916 only 6,500 Coventry men had enlisted, it was claimed. The appropriate figure, based on population, should have been about 10,000 and papers like the *Coventry Graphic* blamed a failure of leadership in the city, by which they meant employers who were reluctant to encourage men to enlist with so much work available.

For months there had been complaints that some young men in Coventry would only consider answering the nation's call if they could become officers, a perception that had prompted the *Graphic* to use a photograph of the ruined Cloth Hall at Ypres, with a caption that read, 'Just a reminder to some of the young

Coventry soldiers from the 1/7 Warwickshires in a relaxed mood.

NOW THEN, YOU.

Look here, my lad, if you're old enough to walk out with my daughter, you are old enough to fight for her and your Country.
At any Post Office you can obtain the address of the nearest Recruiting Office.

men of Coventry. How would they like to wake up and find St Mary's Hall like this?'

In December 1915, the workforce at the Swift Motor Company downed tools because there were still young single men working there who had shown little interest in joining up.

Time to enlist, young man.

Compulsory Service

It was a pattern not confined to Coventry. The attritional battles of 1915 had blown away the British Army's seasoned professionals and Kitchener's eager volunteers and there were simply not enough recruits coming forward to replace them. Some way of forcefully 'encouraging' enlistment would have to be found, in spite of the bluster of blowhards like Horatio Bottomley, editor of the *John Bull* newspaper, who in a speech at Coventry

Hippodrome earlier in the year had assured his audience that compulsory service would never be needed in Britain. This was a country, he bellowed, in which two million free soldiers were the equivalent of twenty million anywhere else in the world.

The government's first move, in the late autumn of 1915, was to introduce the Derby Scheme, named after Kitchener's new Director General of Recruiting, Edward Stanley, 17th Earl of Derby. This required every eligible single man between the ages of 18 and 41 not in an essential occupation, to make a public declaration that he was willing to fight and would attend a recruiting office within forty-eight hours.

It produced more than 300,000 medically fit new recruits, but there was evidence that almost two-fifths of potential servicemen were still refusing to enlist. And so in February 1916 a Bill was rushed through Parliament to introduce conscription, at first for single men in that 18 to 41 age bracket, and then in May for married men.

In Coventry, the prospect of conscription being extended to married men prompted an angry protest meeting at the Empire Theatre, during which an audience of more than 2,000 husbands demanded a pledge from the government that every eligible single man would be conscripted before they were.

The strength of feeling was understandable. Steadily mounting casualties revealed a heart-breaking story of anguish among many families in the city. For at least a year, the wives and mothers of men missing on the battlefields had been placing appeals in local newspapers for news of their loved ones, who'd often been missing for months.

Private William Arthur Jeffs of the Gordon Highlanders had not been heard of for seven months when in July 1915 his mother appealed for news of him in the *Coventry Graphic*. Young Jeffs, aged just 16 and from North Street in the Stoke area of Coventry, was never seen again. It turned out he'd been killed in action in December 1914 and his body had never been found.

In another agonising twist to the grim tale of casualties, each week throughout the spring of 1916 local newspapers carried photographs of sweethearts that had been picked up from the

WHOSE PHOTOS ARE THESE ?

PICKED UP AT YPRES.

Three weeks ago we reproduced two photos which had been picked up by a Coventry soldier on the battlefield of Ypres. One of these—that of the lady—has since been claimed, but no one has recognised the photo of the soldier. This week we have received from another Coventry soldier at the Front two more photos which have been found near Ypres. They bear evidence that they were taken in Coventry, and we shall be pleased to hand them to the owners. Claims must be made personally at the Graphic office, St. Mary Street.

Photographs from the battlefield. They were often claimed by the bereaved.

bodies of the fallen on battlefields. Each was accompanied by an appeal for the young woman in the picture to come forward and claim the photograph. And in a dignified, anonymous way, many did.

A Thin Line

On 21 April 1915, Foleshill-born Albert Troughton, a private in the Royal Welch Fusiliers, wrote a final letter home to his mother:

> I am sorry to tell you that we are to be shot tomorrow at seven o'clock in the morning. Mother, don't be angry with me because I have gone to rest, and pray for me and I will pray for you. I am only a common soldier and all civilians should know I have fought for my country in hail, rain and sunshine. I shall die like a soldier, so goodbye.

Troughton had joined the army in 1911, serving with the 1st Battalion, Royal Welch Fusiliers in Malta. On 23 October 1914, in savage fighting around the village of Zandvoorde near Ypres, the battalion was outflanked by German infantry and enfiladed by artillery. In the chaos, Private Troughton went missing – and was finally arrested five months later by a suspicious French policeman in a café in Calais.

At his courtmartial for desertion, his only defence was that he had heard that one of his three brothers serving with the colours had been killed and that it had turned him 'quite silly'. 'I wandered about France and didn't know where I was going,' he said. First Army Commander General Alexander Haig remained unimpressed and recommended the firing squad.

Like Troughton, Arthur Hutt had been a peacetime soldier, in his case joining the Territorials of the 7th Battalion, Royal Warwickshire Regiment in 1909.

After serving in the front line for the first year of the war, he returned to his job at Courtaulds in Coventry, but by the autumn of 1917 was back in the battalion, going into action in what became known as the Battle of Passchendaele.

On 4 October 1917 at Terrier Farm, south-east of Poelcapelle, when all the officers and NCOs of his platoon had become casualties, Private Hutt took command. Held up by a German strongpoint, he ran forward and killed an officer and three men, forcing forty to fifty others to surrender. Later, he pulled the platoon back, sniping to cover their withdrawal and carrying in a badly wounded comrade. After consolidating the position he went out under heavy fire and one by one carried back to safety another four men.

For his heroism, Arthur Hutt was awarded the Victoria Cross, the first native-born Coventrian to win the coveted medal. Asked later why he'd done it, he said he'd just heard that his brother Bertie had been wounded, fatally as it turned out, and was angry.

In the maelstrom of the trenches, the line between heroism and desertion could be paper thin.

A proud Mrs Troughton and her four sons. Albert is second from the left.

COURTESY OF MARK RADFORD

Battle of the Somme

Coventry's newspapers greeted with some excitement the news that the eagerly anticipated Big Push had at last begun on 1 July 1916, but by the end of the month their columns were beginning to reflect first news of 'terrible casualties'.

The Royal Warwickshire Regiment was already sustaining severe losses, even though the battalions of particular interest to Coventry, the 1/7 and 2/7, were not involved in that first day of the Battle of the Somme, during which the British Army suffered 57,000 casualties.

A view of the Battle of the Somme that did not reflect reality.

COURTESY OF MARK RADFORD

By permission of "Punch."

WELL DONE, THE NEW ARMY !

One horrified witness of that day, the worst in British military history, was Captain Leslie Aldridge, who had enlisted in the 4th South Midland Howitzer Brigade in the city after seeing a recruitment poster in the window of the *Coventry Standard* newspaper office.

Recalling his experience more than twenty years later, he wrote, 'All the lessons learned in the South African war about taking cover were forgotten. I still wonder why our troops were forced to attack as they did.'

By mid-July the 1/7 battalion had seen action and suffered casualties in the Ovillers section of the battle-front, but it was to be the 2/7 who suffered hardest, principally during a failed diversionary attack at Fromelles on 19 July.

As the battalion war diary laconically observed, 'The attack began at 6 p.m. and withdrawal began at 8.10 p.m. The Germans have manned their front lines and those who went over first are no more.'

In this one attack the 2/7 lost thirteen officers and 370 men were killed, wounded or missing. Among them was Coventry-born Captain Thomas Henry Bethell, aged 31, a former barrister, who was shot in the head leading his D Company in a charge on the second line of German trenches.

Also among the fallen was 28-year-old Sergeant Christopher Bailey, formerly a clerk with the Coventry Chain Company, who was last seen with ten of his men in the German trenches.

Against the names of four Coventry men who fell that day stands an intriguing question mark. Lance-Corporal Henry Charles Davenport, a former butcher aged 21; Privates 19-year-old Alfred Lamb; George Albert Taylor, a driller aged 20; and Aubrey Topp, a 27-year-old builder, were each recorded as having died on 19 July while a prisoner-of-war. What that means isn't clear. Did they die later as POWs who had been captured that day, or were they killed by cross-fire in the heat of the action?

The savagery of the Battle of the Somme claimed the lives of many Coventry men serving in other regiments, among them Cecil Arthur Mountfort Iliffe, who, despite coming from a prominent Coventry family and being a Cambridge graduate,

> The official figure for the number of Coventry men killed in the Great War stands at 2,587. The true figure of those whose lives were shortened by it will never be known.

was serving as a private in the 9th Battalion, Royal Fusiliers when he died on 13 August 1916.

Iliffe, whose father was a manufacturer of cords or tyres in the city, was intending to become an Anglican priest and had attended theological college before postponing his ordination to join the army.

Another Coventry soldier who had opted for service in the ranks rather than seeking an officer's commission was Roland Mountfort, a former pupil of King Henry VIII School, whose father and grandfather had both been bank managers in the city.

Born in Coventry in 1890, Mountfort had moved to London before the war to work for the Prudential Insurance Company and in early 1915 joined the 10th Battalion, Royal Fusiliers, dubbed the 'stockbrokers' battalion.

He was wounded at Pozieres on 16 July 1916 and in a letter written the following day he evoked with somewhat heavy-handed sarcasm the all-pervading Big Push fever to describe what happened:

> We tried a push ourselves yesterday morning. I hadn't pushed far before a machine gun pushed a bullet through my shoulder as I pushed up. A bullet hit my right shoulder just at the top and came out several inches lower down my back, a nice, clean flesh wound. I lay in a shell hole for a couple of hours and then made my way back. I have had an absolutely negligible quantity of pain.

After recovering from his wound in England, Mountfort was posted to Africa with a different Fusiliers battalion. He survived the war, only to die of cancer at the early age of 40 in 1930.

Further Afield

As the war spread out from the stalemate of the trenches in northern Europe, it took many Coventry men with it.

One of them was Walter Mealand, later in life a solicitor in Coventry, but at the time a sergeant in the Warwickshire

Yeomanry. This was the Territorial cavalry unit that had been first in the parade to march past when King George V reviewed the 29th Division at Stretton-under-Fosse in March 1915.

Mealand, who'd joined the Yeomanry at the age of 18 in 1912, was with the 1/1st squadron when they landed at Suvla Bay on the Gallipoli peninsula in August 1915 and fought as dismounted infantry. Recalling the campaign more than twenty years later, he remembered with a shudder the torment of the flies and heat.

Decimated by disease and protracted attacks on the Turkish defenders, barely a dozen Warwickshire Yeomanry were left standing out of the original 550 when the unit was finally withdrawn to Egypt and thrown into the campaign against the Turks in Palestine and the Sinai Desert.

During the Third Battle of Gaza, Mealand took part in one of the last cavalry charges in British military history, one of 170 men of the Warwickshire and Worcestershire Yeomanry who charged artillery and machine guns manned by Turkish and Austrian soldiers at Huj.

They lost twenty-six men and 100 horses in the charge, which has been compared to the Charge of the Light Brigade in the Crimea. But they were successful in over-running the guns and thereby removing an obstacle to the final British victory under General Allenby.

Mealand's own memories of this momentous action were blunt. 'As we charged with drawn swords towards the guns, all we could see were banks of smoke and fire, not a man visible. We simply went on and through and then came back for the gunners.'

Dramatic events had not finished with Walter Mealand. As he and his Yeomanry comrades set out for the return journey to France in May 1918, the transport ship they were travelling on, the HMT *Leasowe Castle*, was torpedoed by U-boat 51, 100 miles out of Alexandria, with the loss of more than ninety men. Among those drowned was Private Ambrose Cole who lived at Spon End post office, a former Bablake School pupil.

It was not in fact the Yeomanry's first brush with the war at sea. In April 1915, as they had set sail for Gallipoli, the ship carrying their horses, the steamer *Waverley*, had been torpedoed

Horses being prepared for evacuation on the steamer Waverley.

by a U-boat north of the Scilly Isles. On that occasion the ship stayed afloat and due to the bravery of a number of Yeomanry soldiers, 763 horses were safely put ashore.

Another Coventry soldier whom the war found serving thousands of miles from home was Lieutenant Arthur Meyrick Bones, nephew of Triumph founder and Mayor of Coventry, Siegfried Bettmann.

Bones had had a troubled and restless youth, finding himself expelled from at least one school and failing to knuckle down to a position in the Triumph Company that his uncle had found for him.

Before the war, he'd taken himself off to South Africa to join the imperial police and when hostilities broke out he enlisted in the South African Mounted Rifles, later finding himself attached to the King's African Rifles. He seemed to have finally found his feet, writing to the school magazine of King Henry VIII School in August 1916, 'Our natives are top-hole; they are keen as anything on killing something German. I expect this show will be over in a few months, but I want to stop up here if possible. It is a lovely country with all kinds of wild game in it.'

It wasn't to be. Bones was killed just weeks later, in a German attack on British positions at Iringa in what is now Tanzania.

For Gunner Sidney Onslow, who had joined the Royal Artillery as a trumpeter aged 13, the first serious threat to life and limb came not in continental Europe but in Ireland, where in 1916 his battery had been sent as part of the British response to the Easter Rising.

Onslow and some comrades were in a bar in Dublin one night when they realised that a group of men staring at them were Sinn Féin volunteers and meant them real harm. As the soldiers fled, Onslow was shot in the heel by one of the Republicans but managed to escape.

Later wounded by shell fire at Armentières, Onslow survived the war and went on to carve a career for himself between the wars as comedian and 'burlesque performer' Syd Starr, a well-known figure in his native Coventry.

Another who survived the war to contribute to the city's cultural life was composer and musician Charles Leeson, a compositor with the *Coventry Standard* newspaper before the war, who'd joined up in September 1915.

Leeson, a signaller with the 2/7 Royal Warwickshire Regiment, landed in France in August 1916 and by December found himself undertaking the highly risky business of going out into No Man's Land under shellfire to mend breaks in the barbed wire.

Over its wartime service in France and later in Italy, the 1/7 battalion of the Royal Warwickshire Regiment lost around 420 men. The 2/7 battalion's losses in France and Flanders were even greater, amounting to around 570.

In January 1917 he joined the 61st Division Concert Party as pianist and spent the next twelve months writing and performing religious music and marches for shows and church services behind the lines. But in March 1918, as the German Army threw everything into a last desperate offensive on the Western Front, he was attached to a casualty clearing station right in the midst of the fighting. 'This has been the most terrible day I have experienced in my life,' he wrote to his brother, recalling his work receiving the wounded on 21 March. 'If I could have got away into solitude, I would have wept bitterly.'

Leeson, clearly a sensitive individual, had seen the worst that artillery and machine guns could do to fragile human beings, and one Coventry soldier who knew the truth of that was Lance-Sergeant Henry Craven of the 6th Battalion, East Kent Regiment, The Buffs who'd been badly wounded in 1915 and invalided back to England.

Craven, a former civil servant, took to poetry to describe his feelings and his 'Soliloquy of a Disabled Soldier' was published in the February 1916 issue of *The Wheatleyan*, the school magazine of Bablake School, where he had been a pupil. It began:

No more except in dreams
Or in those haunting visions of the past
Which soon dissolve in air, yet while they last
Bear all the imprint of reality,
Hear we the roar and thunder of the guns,
Or grimly wait at break of day the Huns'
Blind onrush towards Eternity.

No more shall we at night
By cloud-veiled moonbeams misty light
Bury in earth the silent dead, or bear
The wounded comrades, groaning back to where
There's healing and security.

The poem continued for another five verses and ended on an optimistic note. However, by the time it was printed, Craven had recovered from his wounds and been sent back to the front line, where he was killed in action on 6 March.

In the Air

One of Coventry's earliest and youngest flyers was former apprentice engineer Harold Jackson, of The Spring, Stoke, who qualified as a pilot and applied for a commission in the Royal Flying Corps in May 1915. Captain Jackson, as he became, was killed in action at the age of 21 on 7 June 1917, the first day of the Battle of Messines near Ypres, when his machine was hit by a high-explosive shell, blowing off one of his feet. He managed to land but died of his wounds shortly afterwards.

Jackson wasn't the only Coventry-born pilot killed in action, but most deaths occurred from accidents as the crude and developing technology of aircraft was asked to cope with the rigours of combat. Second Lieutenant Herbert Nelson, of the Royal Naval Air Service, son of the Rudge-Whitworth Works manager in Coventry, was one victim, losing his life in March 1918 when his machine suddenly nosedived into the ground at Hemel Hempstead in Hertfordshire.

Closer to home, a number of deaths were associated with the aerodrome constructed on fields alongside the Daimler Works in Radford and designated in May 1915 as No. 1 Aircraft Acceptance Park, from where aircraft prepared for active service were dispatched to their squadrons.

The first aeroplane made by Daimler prepares for its maiden flight.

COURTESY OF THE HERBERT HISTORY CENTRE

The Chief Constable of Coventry's wartime annual reports spelled out the death toll – six in 1917, another five the following year – yet few resulted in a full public inquest, an omission that in hindsight smells of a cover-up.

The reasons for official secrecy might be deduced by the reminiscences of Air Marshal Sir John Higgins, who had served as a senior brigade commander in the Royal Flying Corps in the First World War. Speaking in retirement in Leamington Spa in the late 1930s, he recalled one close shave as he took off from Radford after inspecting some new aircraft produced by Daimler:

> Because of the wind, I had to take off in the direction of houses. Just as I got into the air and when I could not possibly turn back the engine suddenly stopped. The only thing I could look forward to was crashing on to the houses. But just as I was anticipating disaster, the engine suddenly picked up again and I was able to skim the roofs of the buildings in safety.

The rush to improve aircraft performance with new and innovative engines was creating an extra hazard in what was already a dangerous activity. Engine cut-outs were not uncommon and in an age when an RFC pilot's safety equipment did not include a parachute, he had little option but to stay with the machine.

5

Keep the Home
Fires Burning

Writing to a Coventry newspaper in November 1916, one former resident took a highly jaundiced view of the wartime city on his first return in a decade: 'As it stands, Coventry is a city which would fail to impress any newcomer with a desire to remain indefinitely,' he wrote, lambasting its 'dingy shops in narrow, dirty and cancerous streets, its hundreds of tumble-down buildings and so-called garden suburb.'

Quite a put-down for a place that had recently been described in a book on Warwickshire poetry as 'England's Bruges'. Yet not every visitor was as unkind.

Wounded soldiers in the gymnasium at Courtaulds.
COURTESY OF DAVID FRY

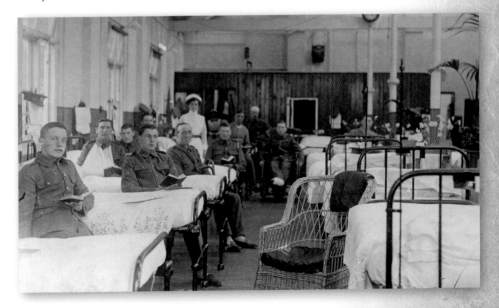

Lance-Corporal John Oliver of the Royal Scots, recovering in a Coventry hospital that summer from wounds received during the early stages of the Battle of the Somme, found the city an intriguing place, a 'curious blending of medieval and ultra-modern'.

Oliver was one of almost 5,000 wounded soldiers who were sent to hospitals in Coventry for treatment and convalescence during the war.

The Coventry and Warwickshire Hospital, placed on a war footing by the end of 1914, accounted for half of them, while two Voluntary Aid Detachment (VAD) hospitals, so-called because they were staffed by volunteers, treated around a thousand each.

One VAD hospital was established in Courtaulds' company gymnasium in Matlock Road. The other was located at Hillcrest, a large house on Barr's Hill in Radford, formerly owned by the Bethell family. It stood next door to the old Starley family home, itself recently converted into a girls' school.

Hillcrest was opened in mid-January 1915 to treat the sick from the Royal Munster Fusiliers and South Wales Borderers, who had just arrived in the city from service in the Far East, and by May had acquired an open-air ward – a bracing dose of fresh air was regarded as an aid to recovery.

From the start, Hillcrest attracted Coventry's middle class to work as volunteers. Dr Walter Brazil, brother of the famous children's writer Angela, was among its medical staff, while its nursing helpers included a Miss Hillman, two Miss Rotherhams, a Mrs Cash and a Mrs Pridmore.

Another prominent Coventry couple, Mr and Mrs Walter Phillips, created a convalescent home for soldiers in a wing of their home, The Grange in Davenport Road, Earlsdon, said to be the biggest private house in Coventry at the time.

There was also the smaller Longford Naval Hospital, established in the twelve-room vicarage of St Thomas's church in Hurst Road, Longford, and run by the vicar, the Revd W. Dore Rudgard. By the end of the war it had dealt with 135 patients.

It has become a truism of the Great War that shell shock was not treated but punished, yet there were wounded soldiers in Coventry at the time who suffered from just that condition and who had apparently escaped censure. In August 1916 city newspapers reported two cases of recovery from the effects of shell shock, both involving the power of speech.

A Private Durrant of the Royal Fusiliers, being treated for shell shock at the Courtaulds Hospital, was said to have recovered his power of speech as he laughed at the antics of Miss May Henderson, the Dusky Comedy Queen, at the Coventry Hippodrome.

A few days later, a Coventry soldier, Private K. Sadler of the 1/7th Royal Warwickshire Regiment, who had been discharged from the army after being treated at four hospitals and given up as a hopeless case, suddenly recovered his power of speech when he burst into song during a musical evening with friends at home in Lansdowne Road in Hillfields.

Private Durrant and the artiste who helped him recover his voice.
COURTESY OF MARK RADFORD

An Inspiring Teacher

In November 1914, a Coventry headmistress wrote proudly in her school logbook of her pupils' contribution to the war:

> The girls have completed a large consignment of specially knitted socks with heels and toes strengthened to resist hard wear and have sent them to the Warwickshires at the front. Each pair contains a scholar's letter, four bars of chocolate and ten cigarettes.

Attending to the bodily comforts of soldiers at the front was one thing, but Selina Dix's real mission was to improve the lives of the girls and their families, some of the poorest in Coventry, among whom she had lived and worked for more than twenty-five years.

Born in Beeston, Nottingham in 1859, the daughter of a lace machine smith, Selina qualified as a teacher in Lincoln and in 1889 moved to Coventry to become head of the girls' department of South Street School in Hillfields. Four years later she was appointed headteacher of the girls' department of the newly built Wheatley Street School, an educational establishment whose innovative attainments would attract visitors from as far afield as Norway, South Africa, China and the United States.

Under Selina's guiding hand, the school's curriculum was broadened to include the teaching of French and visits to places of historic interest. She also pioneered work in domestic science, including instruction in diet, physiology and hygiene, amongst her pupils and their families.

During the war, she promoted communal kitchens and set up a cookery centre at Wheatley Street to improve the well-being of families struggling to cope. She also broadened the range of her active concerns to include the children of bargee families on Midlands canals and Belgian refugees in Coventry, turning a group of young Belgian children made fractious and disorderly by their terrible ordeal into well-motivated and high-achieving pupils.

Girls at Wheatley Street School knitting socks for the Warwickshires.

In the autumn of 1918, she was awarded the MBE for her inspirational welfare work on behalf of women and children in Coventry and was asked by the National Union of Teachers to stand for Parliament under their auspices in the first General Election to give women the vote.

A member of the union's National Executive since 1907, she turned down the opportunity, citing physical frailty, but even after her retirement in 1924, Selina Dix remained a powerful and active advocate on behalf of the poor and dispossessed. From her modest home in Fairfax Street, she continued to offer advice and support to the people of Hillfields right up to her death in 1942.

A Question of Conscience

In the late summer of 1916, Arthur Henry Feast, a fruiterer and vegetable salesman from Kingston Road in Earlsdon, appeared before a Coventry Military Tribunal seeking exemption from service in the army on the grounds that he was a conscientious objector.

Feast, who had been in business for ten years, said he had attended meetings of the Christadelphians, although he was not a member of that movement, and shared their opposition to military service. He offered to give three hours a day to work on behalf of the community, as long as it was not in a workplace where munitions were produced.

His chances of success must have appeared slim, just weeks after the appalling sacrifices made by some of his fellow citizens on the Somme. In addition, the tribunals were typically an authoritarian mix of local worthies, long-serving city councillors and 'military representatives' who were often members of the local gentry.

Oddly though, the tribunal accepted Feast's offer and gave him total exemption, on condition that they could check each month that he was keeping his word.

Another tribunal had been much less understanding back in March when schoolmaster H.D. Ryder, from Alderman's Green, sought exemption from military service on the grounds that he was a Wesleyan who wanted no part in the war and was not willing to consider service in a non-combatant role in the Royal Army Medical Corps.

It may be that Ryder was a little forceful in making his case, for the tribunal not only dismissed his appeal out of hand, but wrote to the school where he worked and to the city's Education Committee demanding that a man with such views should not be allowed to teach children and should be sacked forthwith.

Opponents of the war had been careful to hide their views in the first two years of the conflict, but on 29 November 1916 there was a strong turnout for the anti-conscription campaigner Philip Snowden MP when he spoke at a meeting in Coventry.

In many places such meetings had to be clandestine, but Coventry's Chief Constable, Charles Charsley, gave it his full approval on the understanding that the audience raised a collection for the Coventry Police Fund, a charity helping the families of officers serving in the war.

The towering Charsley – he was 6ft 4in – was an unusual figure for a senior policeman. He had been a professional footballer before joining the force in his native Birmingham and in 1893 had played in goal for England against Ireland.

He was a man of liberal sentiments, doing all he could to ensure German aliens in Coventry were fairly treated and checking the wilder excesses of those who wished to parade their patriotism in a vengeful way.

Policing the City

The wartime city that Charsley was policing enjoyed a declining suicide and road accident rate but had to deal with a rising rate of deaths at work (fourteen in 1916), due to what the Chief Constable called in his annual report for that year the 'abnormal conditions' of munitions production.

The city was generally free of serious crime, although there were three murders in 1915, the only year of the war for which murders were reported. The most sensational happened in September, when a young woman named Louisa Carver was found with her throat cut in a house in St John's Street. Her killer, Private John McCue of the Royal Irish Rifles, admitted the crime but said he couldn't remember doing it. In his defence it was said that he had fought in the Battle of Mons the year before and been wounded five times.

Ten Coventry police officers were to lose their lives on active service and by June 1917 Charsley had taken the radical step of recruiting women officers, two initially, to help police a city that was home to thousands of young women engaged in war work.

'The experience of appointing policewomen has been amply justified by the results,' he concluded in his annual report. 'The work of policewomen is mainly preventive and the amount of good already achieved is considerable. They are in touch with all the social workers in the city and the welfare workers in the

Women police officers form an honour guard as Queen Mary arrives in Coventry.

COURTESY OF DAVID FRY

factories and have an intimate knowledge of the various clubs and hostels provided for the welfare of women and girls.'

In the public mind, women police officers were also ideally placed to deal with what appeared to be an alarming wave of juvenile delinquency in the city in 1917. Indictable offences for the year rose from ninety-one to 302, most of them committed by juveniles.

Once again Charsley showed a relaxed attitude to the crisis that seems liberally modern in outlook. 'Personally, I see no cause for alarm in the increase', he wrote. 'The times are abnormal and children are left much to their own resources, and many possess an inventive genius, so far as mischief is concerned. They may steal but often throw away articles they have stolen.'

Hearth and Home

The physical health of the city's children, rather than their moral well-being, was the focus of concern for Coventry's forceful Medical Officer of Health, Dr Hugh Snell.

His annual report for 1915 recorded the opening of the Corley Camp for Delicate Children, which by October had accommodated twenty-seven of Coventry's most fragile youngsters, and commented in depth on the work of the medical inspection regime over which he presided.

It had thrown up the odd surprising statistic, for example finding that at the age of 13 girls in Coventry were taller and heavier than boys, but had also uncovered some more worrying trends. Of the 2,400 children examined, more than fifty per cent had some defective teeth.

Snell seems to have taken a keen, but not always sympathetic, view of parental care, describing as 'overdressed' one little boy who came forward for inspection wearing a woollen vest, a cotton vest, a flannel shirt, a waistcoat, a coat lined with flannel and an overcoat.

But he acknowledged particular areas of concern, reporting that of the 141 canal boats inspected to investigate family living conditions, thirty-three had infringed public and health legislation. And he recognised that in a city bursting at the seams, overcrowding presented hazards of its own to public health. In 1915, for example, there were almost as many deaths from measles as from cancer.

Coventry's chronic housing shortage, a cause for concern even before the war, had worsened considerably as the insatiable demand for munitions turned medium-sized companies into leviathans. In one case reported to the authorities, seventeen people were found to be living in one cottage in Foleshill.

At first, attempts to get to grips with what at its simplest was a shortage of beds appeared fairly desperate, as schools, a disused skating rink and even sections of the Coventry workhouse were hurriedly turned over to billets for those building, and working in, factories.

The Corley Camp for Delicate Children.

COURTESY OF MARK RADFORD

In 1921, it was reported that during the war only 828 homes had been built by the city council, with another 427 constructed by the Ministry of Munitions. Coventry was still short of more than 2,000 homes.

In December 1915, under pressure from the government, the Chamber of Commerce and the city council fell out over who should co-ordinate the provision of new housing. But by the end of the year the council was making preparations to build a new housing estate of 600 homes on 50 acres of virgin countryside at Stoke Heath for the workforce of the Coventry Ordnance Works.

Built at a cost of £201,000, most of it met by a government grant, the houses were to be the last word in spacious modernity, boasting three bedrooms and an indoor toilet. They were ready for occupation before the end of 1916, a breakneck pace of construction that later in the war would come back to haunt landlord and tenants alike.

Fear and Fun

One solution to the housing shortage.

COURTESY OF MARK RADFORD

Life for the foot soldiers in Coventry's army of munitions workers was an exhausting grind of long hours and ferocious production targets, but there were diversions.

HOW THE PROSPERITY OF COVENTRY CAN BE INCREASED.

The reputation of Coventry-made Goods is famous the World over. All the Nations of the World are crying out for Coventry's manufactures. To meet this demand, every worker must be encouraged to put forth his best efforts towards speeding up production, and every firm and factory in Coventry must increase its army of operatives.

HOW CAN YOU EXPECT TO SWELL THE RANKS OF YOUR WORKPEOPLE IF THERE IS NO ACCOMMODATION FOR THEM
∴   ∴   IN YOUR LOCALITY?   ∴   ∴

The deficiency can only be made good if you subscribe to the fullest possible extent to

6% LOCAL BONDS.
THE SIMPLEST AND SOUNDEST INVESTMENT.

APPLY TO—
The City Treasurer's Department, The Council House, Coventry.

Rudge Whitworth's women footballers.
COURTESY OF DAVID FRY

While sport at the top level had been suspended for the duration of the conflict, there were still opportunities for those so minded on the football field – for both sexes. Women's football thrived during the war, led by companies like Humber and Rudge who fielded powerful teams of female munitions workers, drawn from all over the country.

The ranks of Coventry's fledgling cinemas had been strengthened in the first autumn of the war by the opening of a plush new picture house, The Globe in Primrose Hill Street, complete with seats of crimson velvet and an entrance that featured imposing marble steps beneath an ornamental glass cover.

Coventry's theatres, led by the Hippodrome, were still doing good business and could still attract some of the country's top performers. In late October 1916 the comedian T.E. Dunville, one of the biggest stars of the pre-war music hall, topped the bill twice nightly for a week to packed houses and huge acclaim.

This wasn't entirely surprising. Thomas Edward Wallen, to give him his real name, was Coventry born and bred, leaving the city as a teenager to pursue his ambitions on the stage. His next appearance in his native city, in December the following year, coincided

Coventry's own music hall star T.E. Dunville.
COURTESY OF KEITH RAILTON

T. E. Dunville.

with a speaking engagement at the nearby Opera House for the famous suffragette Christabel Pankhurst, who was touring the country making speeches in support of the war effort.

Zeppelin Fears

In truth, the war was never far away, even as people were relaxing and enjoying themselves. On 1 February 1916, a performance of Verdi's opera *Il Trovatore* at the Opera House had to be conducted by cycle lamps after a Zeppelin scare caused the switch to be thrown on the house lights.

Fear of Germany's super-weapon had already turned Coventry into what many believed was the country's 'darkest city', with draconian regulations governing the showing of lights at night. In early 1916 these even snared the city's Mayor, Councillor Malcolm Pridmore, who was fined 40s by magistrates for having improperly lit lamps on his motor car. Later that spring two city vicars found themselves in the dock for showing lights in their churches.

Whitewashing pavements to help in the blackout.
COURTESY OF MARK RADFORD

A regional warning system for the approach of Zeppelins, crude but moderately effective, more than once shut down munitions factories and plunged streets into darkness. And fears were reinforced in January 1916 by a destructive attack on industrial towns the other side of Birmingham, in which the Lady Mayoress of Walsall, May Julia Slater, lost her life.

Coventry's sole fatality from the Zeppelin menace turned out to be Mary Ann Pegg, a lady in her seventies from Brooklyn Road in Foleshill, who died of shock after the sirens had sounded one night in early March.

The only actual attack on Coventry from the air took place on the night of 12 April 1918, when Zeppelin L62 dropped two bombs, one in the vicinity of the Baginton sewage works, the other in the grounds of Whitley Abbey, where it killed two cows. The target that night had actually been Birmingham and it was a fittingly confused ending for what was almost certainly the last Zeppelin attack on the British mainland.

A Better Weapon

A much more threatening weapon than the vulnerable airship was the U-boat campaign, which by early 1917 was sinking a huge tonnage of cargo ships and steadily bringing Britain closer to the edge of starvation.

The cost of basic commodities like bread, bacon and sugar had risen by nearly fifty per cent since 1914 and wheat prices stood at their highest since 1873. The food shortage was becoming a weapon of war. In Coventry shops ran out of potatoes and citizens took to scavenging in the countryside, where, it was claimed, Warwickshire people were already eating sparrows to supplement their meagre diet of meat.

Amidst deepening official anxiety over food shortages, a National Service Office was opened in the old Town Clerk's offices in Hay Lane and a deputation of Government Food Inspectors arrived in the city, responding to a chorus of complaints about food prices. They found that prices in Coventry were indeed higher than in neighbouring, better-off towns like Warwick, a finding that merely served to heighten a growing clamour for action.

The pressure on families was becoming intense. One young mother wrote to *The Woman Worker* magazine protesting that it was almost impossible to live on the money she earned as prices were rising so fast. She earned 12s 6d for a fifty-two-hour week producing mess tins for soldiers and had to spend a quarter of that paying for her baby to be cared for. Another, with four children, claimed she had just 6s a week left for items like soap, sugar and wool for clothes after paying out for rent, insurance and basic foodstuffs.

Suspicions grew that some were profiteering from shortages. In April 1917, a farmer from Tile Hill, William Reginald Wright, appeared in court charged with watering down milk. The court heard that Wright had taken off in his milk cart when challenged by the city's Chief Food Inspector, W.H. Clarke. Clarke had chased him down on his bicycle, stopped him when the farmer's horse finally ran out of puff, and found that the milk contained almost ten per cent water. He was fined £15.

Food Rationing

Despite regular appeals in the newspapers for people to cut back on foods like bread to preserve stocks, it was clear by the winter of 1917 that rationing was going to be necessary. It came into force in early February 1918, enforcing quantities and prices on basic foods like meat (1s 4d per adult per week), bacon (3oz a week), lard (1oz) and butter or margarine (4oz).

To show that rationing applied even to the highest in the land, children in Coventry schools were given replicas of the Royal Family's ration books to show their parents. Yet suspicions remained.

Shortly after rationing came into force, Alick Hill, managing director of Coventry Chain and Mayor of the city since November 1916, was forced to deny publicly that he was hoarding food, inviting inspectors to rummage through his house, where they found not even enough to support a small household.

To give families access to a more wholesome diet, public restaurants were set up in the kitchen of St Mary's Hall and in Ford Street.

It was a different story in the case of the respected Irish American factory manager Oscar Harmer, right-hand man to Alfred Herbert. When food inspectors raided his home in Spencer Road they found 400lb of tea, 144lb of sugar and thirty-seven tins of salmon. He was prosecuted and sentenced to twenty-eight days' imprisonment and fined £100, later reduced on appeal.

Others took matters into their own hands. Sidney Langford, a labourer, was accused in court of causing a breach of the peace by pushing into a margarine queue outside a shop in Broadgate and calling on the crowd to raid the place. He was bound over to keep the peace, on pain of fourteen days in jail, but his defence was that he had had to wait three hours in the queue, when he had to go to work.

Langford was right to be concerned about timekeeping. Since 1916, tribunals set up under the Munitions of War Act had been rigorous in prosecuting workers who were considered to be 'shirking' or not pulling their weight.

In September of that year, 46-year-old Matthew Lee of Harnall Lane was summoned for neglecting his work at the Dunlop Rim & Wheel Company. It was said he had been absent for six shifts and then was incapable of working. Lee told the tribunal that he was ill with neuralgia, for which he took brandy, but admitted that he was in the pub during the days he should have worked. He was ordered to pay £5 10s in damages.

The intense pressure of munitions work was revealed in the recollections of one anonymous worker employed by Thomas Smith's Stamping Company, a key player in Coventry's frenetic production drive:

> Never was a hammer allowed to stand idle. If a stamper was sick or for any reason could not come to work, his hammer had to be kept going. Many a time I remember after I had done a hard day's work and gone home, a foreman from the stamp shop came to the door to ask me to take another man's place at the hammer. It meant working the full round of the clock but many of us did it often.

> The worst industrial accident of the war was triggered by an old industry, not a new one. On 21 September 1915, a fire deep underground at Exhall Colliery just north of the city killed fourteen miners, most of them from Foleshill.

In the autumn of 1917, a government commission to the West Midlands described munitions workers as 'tired and over-strained', adding that 'the air is very highly charged here and very little will cause a blaze'.

Trouble Ahead

There had already been intimations of trouble ahead in May when more than 15,000 workers in Coventry factories had downed tools in a dispute over 'dilution', the practice that brought women and lower skilled men into jobs formerly reserved for the most skilled.

But it was food shortages and claims of profiteering that provoked the biggest display of outrage. On Saturday 17 November, around 50,000 munitions workers took a day off work and under banners flying the slogan 'To Hell with Profiteers' marched from Pool Meadow to Gosford Green for a massed rally to demand action.

A staggering 50,000 marched in protest of food shortages and profiteers.

COURTESY OF MARK RADFORD

They returned to work on the Monday, but within a week the male workforce at White and Poppe walked out over the issue of shop steward recognition. During the ten-day strike that followed feelings ran high on all sides and in an extraordinary gesture aimed at shaming strikers back to work, aeroplanes dropped leaflets over a demonstration in Broadgate, bearing the words:

Make the Machines!
We Will Fly Them!
Aeroplanes Are Going To Win The War!
The Pilots!

Frightened that industrial conflict would damage the war effort, the government ramped up its propaganda campaign with a new raft of pamphlets aimed at stiffening the sinews of the working man. They included 'An Infantryman's View of Strikes' by one Sergeant H.V. Holmes of the London Scottish, which tried in persuasive fraternal tones to bring strikers on side.

Pilots drop leaflets over a strike meeting in Broadgate.
THE HERBERT EXHIBITION

It had little effect. A further major strike in Coventry factories in late July 1918 attracted furious criticism in local and national press. It coincided with a major Allied push on the Western Front after the German Army's failed Spring Offensive and there were allegations, never substantiated, that enemy agents were behind the strike.

One of the key figures trying to resolve this sudden rash of industrial action in Coventry was a young Daimler trade unionist who had arrived in the city in September 1914 from his native Beeston in Nottingham.

George Hodgkinson was not an out-and-out conscientious objector – he told his foreman that he would join an ambulance unit if he had to – but he did

not agree with the war. He was the only man in the Daimler plant to resist the Derby scheme of attesting for war service and as the company's management tried to get him ostracised, his workmates elected him a shop steward.

Hodgkinson was later elevated to Chief Convener at Daimler, after being the 'instrument of communication' during a three-day sit-in at the company over tool room rates and an abusive foreman that the works committee wanted removed. He also played a key role in bringing to an end the White and Poppe strike of November 1917.

Having turned down the management's offer of a job on the staff as a rate-fixer, working out the price of each job, he also resisted attempts to 'comb' him out, a technique that managements sometimes used to get rid of troublesome union activists by having them drafted into the army.

When he received an official notice to report to Budbrooke Barracks near Warwick, the headquarters of the Royal Warwickshire Regiment, he simply refused, reminding the authorities that he was engaged in vital war work and was allowed to remain where he was.

Hodgkinson's response was polite in comparison to that of fellow trade union official George Williams, who was a prominent member of the anti-war Independent Labour Party and worked at the Coventry Ordnance Works.

When Williams received his call-up papers from the military authorities, he wrote back, 'I am now sitting on the lavatory of the Coventry Ordnance Works and I have your calling-up notice before me. In two minutes, it will be behind me.'

6

COMING HOME

On 7 November 1918, just four days before the Armistice, Private James Thomas Smith of the 4th Battalion, Royal Warwickshire Regiment, was killed in France, aged 20.

Others died of their wounds later, but the former Siddeley-Deasy worker was the last Coventry soldier to be killed in action during the war.

KILLED IN ACTION.

PTE. J. T. SMITH.

Mr. and Mrs. W. H. Smith, 60, Coventry St., Upper Stoke, Coventry, have received the news of the death of their son, Private J. T. Smith, 4th R.W.R. He was killed in action on Nov. 7, 1918; he was 20 years of age, and was formerly employed at the Siddeley-Deasy works, and had only just been married. Smith enlisted in June, 1918, and was sent to France soon afterwards. Another son of Mr. and Mrs. Smith is serving with the R F.A. in Italy.

Private James Smith, the last Coventry soldier to be killed in action.

COURTESY OF MARK RADFORD

Four days later, at lunchtime on Monday 11 November, Councillor Joseph Innis Bates, the city's new Mayor, cut short a visit to Wheatley Street School and with the City Crier at his side drove through the crowds to Broadgate to announce that hostilities had ended.

Factories and schools were closed for the day, bands marched and played and later that evening an effigy of the Kaiser was burned in the streets, but in general the celebrations were muted. Relief was the overriding emotion – that and sorrow for the more than 2,500 Coventry men who would not be returning home.

For the families of prisoners-of-war, the uncertainty and the waiting would go on. The savage battles of the first year of the war had left a surprisingly large number of Coventry men in the hands of the enemy, and by July 1915 their photographs, taken in prisoner-of-war camps like Sennelager in north Germany, were appearing in city newspapers. In early 1916 it was reported that eighty-three Coventry POWs were receiving food parcels sent from home by the Coventry Prisoners' Fund.

The Mayor and Town Crier announce the Armistice in a sea of rejoicing.

COURTESY OF MARK RADFORD

The returning 1/7th Royal Warwickshires at Coventry railway station.

For Private John Watts, a former Humber employee serving with the 1st Battalion, Royal Warwickshire Regiment, the parcels were to prove a lifesaver. In January 1917, Watts penned a vivid account of his captivity for the *Coventry Graphic* from Switzerland, where he had been sent by the Red Cross to recover from a serious illness contracted at Sennelager:

> The first six months in Germany were the worst. We got half-starved, living on cabbage water and black bread, and we got some awful kickings from the sentries. It was nothing to see a German spit in our faces and call us English swine.

Watts escaped and was just 3 miles from the Dutch border when a group of passing children spotted him and his fellow escapees resting in a field and raised the alarm. During the struggle that followed he half-strangled a German soldier and had a rifle butt broken over his head.

Back at the camp he was thrown into prison where a doctor recognised that he was dangerously ill and managed to get him sent to neutral Switzerland. It was the food parcels that saved him from starvation, he said.

For many POWs it was to be December 1918 before they saw Coventry again and in the New Year a civic banquet was laid on in St Mary's Hall for 130 of them.

It was to be 1919 before Coventry's own battalion of Territorials, the 1/7th Royal Warwickshire Regiment, returned to the city. After fighting in the Third Battle of Ypres, the battalion had been sent to Italy, where it took part in the campaign that led to the final rout of the Austrian Army. It suffered serious casualties there, losing, among many others, its Commanding Officer, but its proud boast was that in all its active service it had not had a man taken prisoner.

A Hero's Return

On Saturday, 12 January 1918, crowds gathered in the streets to welcome home the first native-born Coventrian to win the Victoria Cross.

Arthur Hutt of the Royal Warwickshire Regiment, recently promoted to Corporal, was a slightly awkward figure, sitting alongside the Mayor, Alick Hill, in the back of a huge Daimler limousine as it made its way from the railway station into the city centre.

At the Council House, councillors and other prominent citizens bellowed their appreciation as Hutt was presented with a civic gift of £250 in war bonds and carried shoulder-high from the council chamber to greet the crowds outside.

Victoria Cross winner Arthur Hutt with the Mayor, Alick Hill.
COURTESY OF DAVID FRY

White and Poppe's Edward Medal-winning Alfred Henney.
COURTESY OF DAVID FRY

He wasn't the only local hero being lionised that winter. Back in October, Alfred Henney, a senior member of the company fire brigade at the giant munitions works of White and Poppe, had been to Buckingham Palace to receive the Edward Medal, awarded to miners and industrial workers for saving lives in the workplace.

Henney, a former soldier who had been invalided out of the army, had picked up a bucket of detonators that had caught fire and calmly carried it out of the workshops to safety, preventing what could have been an appalling disaster. The Edward Medal, later replaced by the George Cross, was only awarded to 188 industrial workers, making it one of the rarest of British gallantry awards.

Henney was among those presented to Queen Mary during a visit she and Princess Victoria made to White and Poppe on 18 September. Male members of the royal party had to comply with strict factory rules, emptying their pockets of matches, pipes, cigarettes and cigars, or indeed any other material that might be combustible. The Queen, it was reported, did not have to undergo this slightly humiliating process. Presumably, like generations of royals before and since, she carried nothing about her person.

Queen Mary's visit – she was greeted at Coventry Railway Station by the Mayor and escorted to a waiting car through an honour guard of women police officers – was only the second time a senior royal had made it to Coventry during the war.

Central City

It seems paltry acknowledgement of the extraordinary role that the city was playing in supplying the nation with the tools of war. The 'Central City', as the national press dubbed it to preserve its anonymity, was cited as a place where even the clergy rolled up their sleeves and got stuck in.

A reporter from the *London Evening Standard*, sent up to Coventry to gauge the mood, found the Reverend Arthur Wood, a Primitive Methodist minister, turning shells in a munitions factory. Canon Baillie, vicar of St Michael's, was working in the hayfield to free a man for work in the factories, while in the municipal tram sheds Canon Simpson washed trams to release another man to the war effort.

Munitions workers routinely worked from six in the morning until nine at night every day of the week, and until the summer of 1918 most had waived their annual right to take the popular August Bank Holiday off, so that the machines could keep running.

The Tank at Coventry.

Tank D119 rumbles up Hertford Street.
COURTESY OF DAVID FRY

The city itself had undergone enormous physical change during the war, much of it fuelled by the needs of industry. 'Soldiers returning,' commented one newspaper, 'will find Coventry almost unbelievably changed, particularly in areas like Foleshill, where country has turned into town.'

Enthusiasm for the war could still be found. Crowds as big as those for the Godiva processions lined the streets on 10 February 1918 to watch Tank D119 rumble up Hertford Street to Broadgate to act as a rallying point for the sale of War Bonds – the scheme whereby individuals and companies could support the war effort by buying bonds issued by the government. In a week, the city's existing contribution of £621,000, up till then regarded as somewhat disappointing, had more than doubled.

Yet the strains of four years of toil and bereavement were beginning to show. Within weeks of the Queen's visit to White and Poppe, the company's male workforce of around 800 was out on strike because of a perceived threat to shop steward recognition. And even efforts to do something about Coventry's crippling housing crisis began to turn sour.

117

In May 1918, the city council was compelled to meet in special session to discuss residents' complaints about high rents and the poor quality of the houses on the showpiece new Stoke Heath estate. By the end of the year a series of mass public meetings had turned into a rent strike, and even though the council reduced rents by more than a shilling a week and launched an enquiry into shoddy building work, there were threats of another strike if a school was not built to serve the area.

Neither were tensions very far below the surface between Coventry soldiers serving in France and their fellow citizens working in reserved occupations at home. News reaching the front line of strike action among munitions workers invariably prompted the charge of 'shirking' from those in uniform, amid claims that the strikers were somehow sheltering at home while the real work of war was being done elsewhere.

In at least one case, this unfortunate divide led to tragedy. In February 1918, Thomas Alfred Woodward, a married man working as a drop forger at Brett's Stamping works, had a white feather pinned to his front door in Canterbury Street, Hillfields by an unknown hand. Upset at the clear accusation of cowardice, he promptly enlisted, saw action with the Royal Field Artillery in France and died of his wounds on 30 September, at the age of 21.

As the war drew to a close, anxieties were beginning to be expressed about the durability of Coventry's time-honoured apprenticeship system. The war, it was said, had made young people restless. Leaving school at 14, many boys were earning so much money in the factories by the age of 15 that they were unwilling to go back to the usual level of wages paid to apprentices of their age. Even girls only wanted to work in munitions factories.

The nature and complexion of work and its future was clearly going to be a serious challenge for the city to face up to as its men began to return from the war, not in marching battalions paraded through city streets in triumph but in small groups as demobilisation began.

TO MUNITION WORKERS.

YOU are needed for munitions,
  Your Country bids you give
Your whole time and ambitions
  To help your comrades live.

At our Empire's urgent call
  For men and still more men,
You responded one and all
  That our Empire should not fall.

We were needed in the trenches,
  You were wanted at your work,
Some were needed at the benches,
  But none our duties now must shirk.

You have given at work your best,
  We have fought as we were bid ;
Do not plead for a few days' rest,
  Just to spend your well-earned quid.

Have you thought what it will mean,
  To the lads across the way,
If your work for a day you cease,
  Do you know the price you pay.

For without the shells and guns,
  Which we are needing more each day,
'Twould be murder for your gallant sons,
  Who have kept the Huns at bay.

They ask not for a holiday,
  Though they need it every lad,
They ask for shells to pave the way,
  To a great and speedy victory.

Workers to yourselves be true,
  Think not of self awhile,
But heed your armies cry,
  No holidays, but shells, more shells,
  Let shells be your reply.

COPYRIGHT]   Sapper B. G. WINCH, B.E.F.

A soldier's appeal to munitions workers.

A Deadly Contagion

At the height of the epidemic in November 1918, the government took space in local newspapers to issue advice on 'How to Avoid Influenza':

> Always breathe through your nose, never your mouth. Wash the inside of your nose with soap and water, day and night. Make yourself sneeze, night and morning, and do not wear anything tight around your neck. Walk home from work and sleep with the windows open. Don't drug yourself, over-eat or over-clothe yourself. Do not be afraid of flu.

That was easier said than done. Spanish influenza, first detected in the city at the end of June, would kill almost 500 people before it ebbed away at the end of the year.

There was no easy way to avoid it and it killed randomly, taking the young as well as the elderly. More than half of those who died were aged between 20 and 40 and they included fit young men like Perce Kelley from Foleshill, a noted sportsman who had only just enlisted in the Royal Air Force, and William Pickup, aged 34, who had served throughout the conflict as a surgeon in the Royal Navy.

Cases were spread right across the city, irrespective of living standards and social class. The authorities took on extra gravediggers to help with burials but could not find enough nurses to care for the sick.

Action was taken to discourage people from gathering in large crowds. At the height of the epidemic, Coventry's Watch Committee decreed that no children under the age of 14 would be allowed in city cinemas, despite protests from cinema owners. Yet even Coventry's Medical Officer of Health, Dr Hugh Snell, was sceptical about the precautions. 'So little is known concerning how the illness can be averted,' he wrote, 'that it is doubtful to what extent they could have any influence on the spread of the epidemic.'

In the face of such helplessness panic was never far away, and it was plain to see in the case of William Arnold, of Leicester Causeway, brought before the city magistrates on a charge of assaulting a Dr David Holmes.

The court heard that the defendant had appeared at the doctor's house late one evening, asking him if he could visit his ailing daughter. The doctor declined, saying he would visit in the morning, and when pressed said that the girl was not on his list of insured patients anyway. At which point, Arnold struck him on the left temple, knocking him to the floor and breaking his collarbone. It was a serious assault, but the magistrates fined him just £1, because of his obvious distress.

Women's Work

The impact of the soldiers' return was felt most strongly by women. In the munitions factories, theirs had been a long struggle for recognition and fair treatment in the face of employer cynicism and the hostility of established craft unions like the Amalgamated Society of Engineers (ASE).

The ASE, worried that the widespread employment of women would inevitably depress wages generally, had managed, by 1916, to secure a broad agreement that women in government-controlled factories should be paid, for doing the work of a man, £1 for a 48-hour week.

But munitions workers in controlled firms were tied to one factory and had to obtain a 'leaving certificate' if they wanted to switch employers. These were often refused and the Munitions Tribunals who had to adjudicate on cases were not always sympathetic to women.

The struggle for fair treatment that many faced emerges from the transcript of one 1917 Munitions Tribunal, hearing the case against a young woman named Annie Whitfield, who had been sent from Aberdeen to work in Coventry and was living at the Whitmore Park hostels.

Scottish workers brought to Coventry. Is Annie Whitfield among them?
COURTESY OF DAVID FRY

Annie had been summarily sacked for refusing to work a defective machine and it transpired that her wages had also been unfairly docked to pay for her rail fare from Aberdeen. She was told that the deduction would be 2s a week and that it would later be refunded. In fact, it was 7s a week and she was also earning less than she'd been promised. In the words of the Workers' Union organiser George Morris, representing her, she'd been brought to Coventry under false pretences.

On this occasion the tribunal chairman ruled that she should be paid a week's wages and the case adjourned so that the proper rate for the job could be established.

In the vanguard of trying to protect women's interests and improve their pay and conditions were two formidable female trade unionists, Henrietta Givens, Coventry organiser for the National Federation of Women Workers, and Alice Arnold, her counterpart in the Workers' Union, which represented both men and women.

It was Henrietta Givens, later to become Coventry's first woman magistrate, who struck a deal with the ASE's District Secretary, her own husband, Walter Givens, as it happened. She agreed that in return for ASE support, her members would step down at the end of the war when the men came back.

The groundwork for such a tricky manoeuvre was being laid by the winding down of munitions firms like White and Poppe, its huge workforce dominated by women, which in turn signalled a steady exodus from the city of female munitions workers, returning to where they had come from.

Even so, by the beginning of 1919 there were 3,000 women receiving out-of-work support in Coventry, twice the number of unemployed men. The city's Municipal Baths had been converted into a women's department of the Labour Exchange and there was, it emerged, plenty of work to be had in domestic service. Except that domestic service was no longer what the vast majority of women wanted to do. In an impromptu Labour Exchange survey, only five per cent said they would be willing to consider service on a live-in basis, as long as wages and conditions improved. Another twenty-five per cent would consider it if they could live independently, but seventy per cent ruled it out completely.

*A fearful view
of women taking
over men's jobs.*

COURTESY OF MARK RADFORD

NOW THAT WOMEN ARE TAKING THE PLACES OF MEN WHO HAVE
ENLISTED, OUR ARTIST SEES POSSIBILITIES IN THE IDEA.

That refusal to return to what newspapers were already calling 'the drudgery of the kitchen and domestic service' struck a chord, even among the most chauvinist of commentators. Women had proved themselves in the brutally punishing grind of the munitions factories and they had earned the right to nourish ambitions with a real chance of being fulfilled. And that extended to having a vote.

In February 1918, the Representation of the People Act widened the electoral franchise to all men over the age of 21 and to women over the age of 30 who were householders or married to house-holders, or who were graduates voting in a university constituency.

It would be another ten years before women finally gained total parity with men at the ballot box, but in the General Election held on 14 December 1918, a total of 23,618 Coventry women were for the first time eligible to cast a vote.

In the event, the contest for the city's Parliamentary seat was won, with 17,380 votes – almost half those cast – by the Conservative and Unionist candidate Edward Manville, chairman of the Daimler Company. Labour's Dick Wallhead, fresh from a jail sentence for sedition the previous year, was runner-up with 10,298 votes, while bottom of the poll of five candidates, with just 3,145 votes, was the erstwhile Coventry MP D.M. Mason, still shunned by the party he had once represented and forced to stand as an Independent Liberal.

Seven hundred votes ahead of him in the final reckoning was former Coventry soldier Arthur Bannington, a carpenter by trade, who stood on a platform of giving a voice to the discharged servicemen of the city.

THE WAR WORKERS.

"WHAT'S ALL THIS CACKLE ABOUT VOTES AND A NEW REGISTER?"
"DON'T KNOW—OR CARE. WE'RE ALL TOO BUSY JUST NOW."

Women's suffrage. By 1918 even reactionaries had accepted it.

COURTESY OF MARK RADFORD

Future Uncertainties

While many returning soldiers slipped back relatively easily into their old jobs, the struggle of others to find a living was not made easier by the air of uncertainty that hung over Coventry's industrial life. How easy was it going to be to switch companies that had been on a war footing for four years back into the sort of production that peacetime demands required?

Over the final two years of the war, the city's manufacturing focus had shifted from manufacturing war-fighting products like shells and bullets to war-winning armaments like tanks, planes and heavy guns. By the autumn of 1918 Coventry firms had turned out more than 6,000 aircraft and 12,000 aero engines, making the city the country's foremost engine producer and the Standard Company, in particular, one of the country's leading manufacturers of aeroplanes.

12 HP
ROVER   £350

THE ROVER COMPANY LTD. METEOR WORKS, COVENTRY
59-61 NEW OXFORD ST, LONDON, W.C.4 16 LORD EDWARD ST, DUBLIN

*An advertisement
for Rover cars
early in the war.
What came next?*

COURTESY OF MARK RADFORD

Coventry's pre-war expertise in vehicle and engine manufacturing had given it an advantage when it came to this switch of emphasis. And the more far-sighted among the city's industrialists were already limbering up for peacetime.

Both the Triumph and Rover companies were accused, in the final months of the war, of turning their thoughts too closely to the sort of products that would follow in peacetime, while the shrewd John Siddeley, whose modest-sized firm had dramatically expanded to make everything from lorries to aircraft during the war years, went further than anyone in assessing where vehicle manufacturing had got to.

In 1918, Siddeley imported into Britain a luxury car made by the American Marmon Company, had it quietly dismantled at his Parkside factory and with his senior engineers had studied it in minute detail in a new design office at his home in Kenilworth.

Siddeley received national recognition for his contribution to the war effort, being made CBE in January 1918, among a raft of honours given to industrialists and senior factory managers. Daimler's Chief Engineer, Algernon Edward Berriman, and Thomas Smith, General Manager of Coventry Ordnance Works, both received the OBE in the same honours list.

Lower down the pyramid, the conflict had cut a swathe through the pre-war workforces of many companies. The Triumph and Gloria companies lost sixty-six dead, Coventry Chain counted forty-seven lost, while in John Siddeley's own firm twenty-six former employees never returned.

Scars of War

A shocking percentage of those who did come back had to try and rebuild their lives in the face of physical, and some cases psychological, scars that were not always visible but were invariably disabling. It was estimated that by the end of the war there were more than 2,000 discharged and disabled servicemen in Coventry.

Back in 1916, the task of trying to support these men back into employment and family life had been shouldered by voluntary organisations like the Coventry Branch of the Soldiers and Sailors Help Society. But in July of that year the Naval and Military War Pensions Act came into force, establishing a pension entitlement of up to 27s 6d a week and setting up local War Pensions Committees to administer the scheme.

In late January 1919, a meeting of the Coventry War Pensions Committee was told that it was receiving between fifty and a hundred letters a day appealing for help. In the twelve months just past it had paid out £25,800, mainly from national resources, and helped more than 3,000 families.

On its register as the new year dawned, it had 2,860 discharged men and 2,846 dependants of those who had died. Under the war pension's scheme, widows received a £5 gratuity and a sliding scale of weekly allowances for children, beginning with 5s for a first child, and 4s and 2d for a second.

When it came to finding training and work for disabled servicemen, Coventry was slower off the mark than its industrial neighbours, Wolverhampton and Birmingham. It was the end of 1919 before the doors opened at a new Government Instructional Factory, based in premises formerly occupied by the Dunlop Company in Alma Street.

Around 260 ex-servicemen, some with artificial limbs, were directed to the factory to receive training in a range of skills, from general engineering, building trades and vehicle building to woodworking, watch-repairing and tailoring. It was to be a year-long course, with a maintenance grant meeting the first quarter and the rest covered by an employer, who would pay a man's wages and ensure that his pension rights were protected.

There were to be technical advisory committees for each trade, whose responsibilities would be to judge a trainee's capacities and find work for him once the course had finished. Amid a general air of optimism, plans were even drawn up to build a block of houses using men involved in the scheme, with materials supplied by the city council.

On 23 November 1919, Foleshill-born firebrand Tom Mann led a silent march of unemployed men to the new Coventry Cathedral to protest government cutbacks in support for those out of work.

Disabled servicemen learning new skills.

COURTESY OF MARK RADFORD

While the instructional factory scheme did have limited success and some disabled servicemen did get back into work, delays in bringing forward real help for those who had sacrificed their health, if not their lives, for the sake of the nation did not improve the public mood in Coventry.

By early summer 1919, newspaper editorials were calling for the city council to come to the aid of discharged servicemen who'd been evicted from their homes because they couldn't pay the rent. When plans were announced for nationally nominated Peace Day celebrations in July, the Coventry branch of the Soldiers and Sailors Federation decided not to take part, in protest at 'unredeemed promises to discharged servicemen and their dependants'.

Celebrating Peace?

The celebrations were intended to be lavish, beginning on the evening of Friday 18 July with massed singing by more than 4,000 schoolchildren on Greyfriars Green. The following day, thousands more children would march through the city, singing hymns, form themselves into human flags in massive displays to celebrate Britain's allies in the war and then make up an enthusiastic audience for simultaneous firework displays on Spencer Park, Radford Recreation Ground and Stoke Green.

But the centrepiece would be a glittering Peace Pageant on Saturday afternoon, highlighting Coventry's long role in history and featuring Lady Godiva in procession, surrounded by more lords and princes than you could shake a banner at.

There was stiff competition among the civic elite to take on the role of characters like Edward, the Black Prince, Leofric, Earl of Mercia and St George in the procession. The organisers advertised for people with horses to join the cavalcade and they were delighted to announce that even Lady Godiva herself had a properly Coventry background. The actress Gladys Mann, chosen for the role, was actually the daughter of a prominent Coventry councillor.

And there lay the rub. In their jostling for front-rank positions they had completely overlooked those who had played the central part in the city's recent history – the soldiers and munitions workers of Coventry. The whole event was designed to look

The Godiva peace procession on Stoney Stanton Road.

COURTESY OF THE
HERBERT HISTORY CENTRE

backwards in back-slapping celebration by those who thought themselves important in Coventry, many of whom had also done well out of the war. And there was going to be trouble.

The procession passed off peacefully enough, but as a fine afternoon turned into evening rain, cancelling at least one of the firework displays, resentment spiralled into mayhem as stone-throwing crowds attacked shops and business premises in Broadgate and the surrounding streets.

One of the first targets was a shop belonging to Alderman Snape, a prominent organiser of the pageant. Another was the King's Head Hotel, long held to be German owned, and the Black Cat café in Broadgate, whose owner pleaded in vain that he was Danish, not German.

A police baton charge scattered a mob smashing plate-glass windows in Hertford Street and the night ended with twenty-four people in hospital, three of them policemen.

Fighting resumed after the pubs closed on Sunday night. A shopkeeper who had lost a son in the war had his business ransacked. There were reports of women rioters using their aprons to collect granite setts from a building site in Market Street to use as ammunition and even Co-op stores came under attack.

After a third night of street skirmishes, only the arrival of strong police reinforcements from Birmingham and soldiers from the Wiltshire Regiment, drafted in from their billets at Radford Aerodrome, finally restored order, leaving more than a hundred people injured, the city centre strewn with broken glass and discarded missiles and damage estimated at £1,000 caused to commercial premises.

At first, the rioting was blamed on a spontaneous spasm of anti-German sentiment from hooligans fuelled by drink, but a different picture quickly emerged. It transpired that rumours of trouble to come were spreading through Coventry factories in the days before the peace celebration. It was even alleged that some shops, particularly jewellers, had had their windows surreptitiously scratched with diamond cutters so that they could be easily pushed in when the moment came.

In wartime Coventry, to call someone 'a German' became the worst insult it was possible to deliver. Spoken in real anger, it invariably provoked a fight.

The *Coventry Graphic*, in an inflammatory editorial, blamed 'men who hid themselves in a munition factory during the war, drawing big money, and are now discontent because they have lost their positions'.

But among the injured in the fighting were at least two young men wearing khaki, while a serving soldier home on leave, John Cashmore, was one of those quickly brought to court and fined for looting in Broadgate.

The war may well have been won. But the peace looked as though it was going to require a good deal more sorting out.

Alderman Snape, one of the pageant's chief organisers.
COURTESY OF DAVID FRY

Boarded-up shops in Broadgate after the riots.
COURTESY OF DAVID FRY

POSTSCRIPT

LEGACY

Coventry's first bishop for 500 years.

To the national press, the announcement in October 1918 that Coventry was to have its own cathedral church and its own bishop, the first for centuries, was fitting recognition for a place that they had come to view as a second Birmingham.

Whether its own citizens liked to think of it in that way is another matter, but the enthronement of the 73-year-old Bishop of Worcester, Huyshe Yeatman-Biggs, as the first modern Bishop of Coventry on Thursday 21 November was widely perceived as the beginning of a new era for the city.

Much-admired St Michael's church, one of England's biggest parish churches, now had a new status and for the first time in nearly 400 years, Coventry could once again call itself a cathedral city.

In other ways too, Coventry's national profile was rising. In February 1918, the Royal Navy brought into service the light cruiser HMS *Coventry*, the fourth to bear the city's name and the first for more than 150 years. The ship would go on to serve as the floating headquarters of the joint Allied Disarmament Commission, meeting at Heligoland, the huge former naval base on the German coast, in July 1920.

*The new
HMS* Coventry,
*the first for a century
and a half.*

COURTESY OF THE
HERBERT HISTORY CENTRE

A City of Ambition?

The war had given Coventry new ambitions closer to home. No city in the country contained a higher proportion of clever artisans, declared one newspaper, and it was high time that education was given a higher priority. Teachers must be better paid and the city needed to make significant improvements to its schools and to its Technical Institute, which had been established in an old textile warehouse in Earl Street, back in 1888.

In 1919, the city council acquired 3 acres of land on the corner of Albany Road and The Butts for a new building, and in 1926 the institute met the qualifications required to become a technical college and changed its name accordingly. Yet it was to be almost a decade before the new college was opened, with more than 3,300 students enrolled.

By then, Coventry led the country in day-release apprenticeships, with 500 registered in 1931, and pressure for the city to have its own university, first advocated in 1920, was intensifying. In the event it was to be another thirty years before that university, confusingly named after the nearby county town of Warwick, would see the light of day.

Colony cottages in Holbrooks, more huts than houses.

COURTESY OF DAVID FRY

Even before the opening of Coventry's new Council House in June 1920, proposals had been drawn up for a new Town Hall

to go with it, capable of seating 2,500 people for events, concerts and meetings. After a public appeal for suggestions from the Town Clerk, George Sutton, a site in Earl Street, close to the Council House, was identified, but it was never built.

The congested nature of Coventry city centre, apparent even before the war, had already led to the revival of traffic improvement schemes that would in time sweep away more of old Coventry, notably the complex of medieval streets around Butcher Row. But the biggest challenge facing those planning the city's peacetime future was housing.

During the war years the city council had managed to build only 828 new homes, with another 427 built by the Ministry of Munitions, although these 'munitions cottages' were more of a hut than a real house. At the end of 1920, it was estimated that Coventry was still short of 2,150 houses. A start was being made with the new Radford garden suburb, but there was bafflement in many quarters that such a wealthy place had a problem with this.

A Wealthy Place

Just how wealthy would not have come as a surprise to many. It was said that so much money had been made in Coventry during the war that nobody had time to count it.

It was reported that the man who minded a machine automatically turning out parts could take home £25 a week and that people involved in other trades, from publicans and piano dealers to tinkers and tailors, had all gone 'munitioneering', leaving their businesses in the hands of their wives.

One city bank manager was quoted as saying, 'Nowhere in England, I feel sure, are there so many people with amounts of earnings from £10,000 to £20,000 made from the war. Even among artisans, the thrifty have savings of up to £2000.'

One company, he added, had opened a bank branch at its works, the only one in the country, into which 600 account holders had poured £129,000 in deposits.

The war had had one little-noticed effect. The number of tramps seen in Coventry had fallen from 1,700 over a year to 1,000. And there were no children among them.

For those who had made real fortunes from the war, the 'war millionaires' as one national newspaper called them, new opportunities were opening up to buy themselves into a different kind of lifestyle with a country estate.

Death duties, staff shortages and the loss of heirs in the war meant that the country's traditional land-owning gentry and aristocracy were increasingly under pressure to dispose of their estates. Among Warwickshire examples was the Bromley-Davenport family, who in 1918 put their estate at Baginton near Coventry up for auction.

For the skilled man in Coventry, the good times continued on into peacetime. The Labour Party in the city came from almost nowhere to win a third of the seats in the 1919 city council elections on the back of a mini boom, recalled many years later by one keen observer of the city's political scene: 'Trade was never so good, wages were never so high, things were never so dear, as they were in Coventry in 1919,' he wrote.

It didn't last. By 1920 Coventry industry had dipped into recession and the struggle of many firms to regain pre-war export markets were not helped by war reparations levelled against Germany. Engineering castings made in German factories were sent over to Britain and made available free to manufacturers, thereby leaving British engineers short of work. The population of the city, just over 142,000 at its wartime peak, had dipped to 128,000 by the 1921 census.

But lessons had been learned. The war had taught many Coventry companies the value of engineering science and of working together. It had given the city a new electrical engineering industry, spearheaded by GEC, destined in time to become Coventry's biggest single employer. On the back of its proven expertise in aircraft manufacture, Coventry also now had two new aerodromes, at Baginton and Whitley, and the bare bones of its own aircraft industry that would go on to become a major player in the city's fortunes until the 1960s.

On the downside, Coventry had acquired a reputation for trade union militancy and strikes, but in the aftermath of the war, when there were major national railway and police strikes, this was not unique.

As its economy recovered, the extraordinary changes wrought by the war on the city gave rise to plenty of heart-searching. While it was being suggested that it was time for a new history to be written of the ordinary folk of Coventry, there were concerns in some quarters about how those who had come to work in munitions and stayed on would be assimilated into the population.

Would they feel like real Coventrians, and what would all the changes mean for the fabric of what had still been before the war essentially a very old town? Chester redeveloped would not be Chester, went the argument, and neither would this new Coventry be Coventry.

Returning Heroes

Amidst these uncertainties, many of the city's returning heroes found themselves adrift, shorn of the comradeship that had sustained them in the military and unable to express their deeper feelings to friends and families who had not shared their experiences.

The more socially aware among Coventry's wealthy elite tried to help, notably Coventry Chain managing director and former Mayor Alick Hill, who in January 1919 announced that he and his wife were raising money to set up social clubs for discharged servicemen.

It quickly became apparent, however, that the men they were trying to help were not looking for largesse, however well meant. They would set up their own clubs with their own money. The first was the Radford Social Club, which opened at Easter 1919, after 'eight great gentlemen' met in a local pub and each put £25 of their own money into starting it up. It quickly became popular in the growing new suburb and moved to new premises in 1937.

Former members of the largely Coventry-recruited South Midland Howitzer Battery launched their own club to 'meet occasionally and continue the comradeship of their fighting days'. In Foleshill, eighteen ex-servicemen put 6s each into the kitty to set up the Parkestone Club, opened in 1921, and the following year the Stoke ex-servicemen's club opened in Clay Lane.

A meeting of the Howitzer ex-servicemen's club.

In Memoriam

With around 2,600 men lost, the question of how Coventry was to remember and commemorate its dead was a priority, the initial response being a string of suburban war memorials, often temporary in nature.

On 12 October 1919, in appalling weather, a crowd of 10,000 people followed a procession from Pool Meadow to a wooden obelisk, erected in one corner of Spencer Park in Earlsdon, on what was intended to be the site of the city's chief war memorial.

It wasn't just the weather that was unkind. Newspaper comments on the occasion was that it was poorly advertised and rushed through and that the obelisk was inferior to a memorial in wood and plaster which had been unveiled on Durbar Avenue in Foleshill a fortnight earlier.

A third memorial was unveiled on Radford Common in December 1919, but all three were regarded as stand-ins while the city pondered how to come up with a permanent solution with which to remember its lost sons.

As early as March 1919, the Mayor, Joseph Innis Bates, had launched a public appeal for ideas. The result was a plan to raise

Unveiling Foleshill war memorial.

COURTESY OF THE
HERBERT HISTORY CENTRE

139

funds by public subscription and purchase 120 acres of prime farmland from the Gregory estate at Styvechale, building a city war memorial there and incorporating it into a new public park, something that had been widely advocated long before the war.

It was controversial. There were many for whom the idea of a public park when many Coventry citizens did not even have a proper roof over their heads was offensive. At £31,000, the purchase price was thought to be excessive, a view only slightly softened when the Hon. A.F. Gregory agreed to hand back £2,000 as his contribution.

Nevertheless, the money was finally raised and on 9 July 1921 the park was opened with festivities that attracted more than 20,000 people.

Six years later, a further appeal raised the funds for a war memorial built in concrete, faced with Portland stone and erected by sixty unemployed former soldiers. It was unveiled on 8 October 1927 by Field Marshal Earl Haig, assisted by Arthur Hutt, Coventry's VC winner, and by Mrs Eliza Bench of Foleshill, who had lost four of her five sons to the war. Under a rule limiting

A novel way of raising money for the city's chief war memorial.

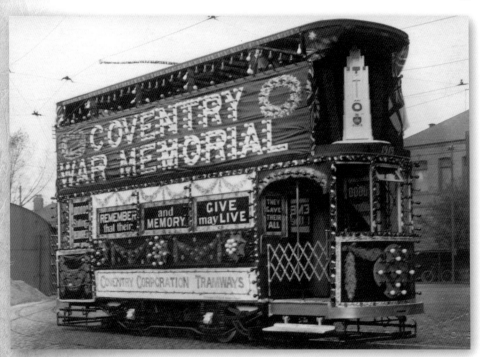

every family to one representative at the ceremony, her husband Joseph was not allowed to accompany her, a cruel twist in the circumstances.

It was an intensely moving event of enormous poignancy, witnessed by a crowd of 50,000 people, many of them veterans. Yet by then the war was beginning to fade into Coventry's back story as the city accelerated into the prosperity and growth that would make it Britain's fastest-growing urban centre between the two world wars.

Memories of Coventry's role in the First World War may have been more carefully nurtured elsewhere. The Germans had never managed to disrupt one of the nation's key munitions centres. While other places, even further from the Zeppelins' home airfields, suffered attack from the air, the super-productive Central City lay hidden beneath its crude blackout and had survived unscathed.

Given a second opportunity some twenty years later, Hitler's military strategists would not make the same mistake again.

BIBLIOGRAPHY

Newspapers and Magazines

Coventry Graphic, 1912–1921

Coventry Herald, 1914–1920

Coventry Standard, 'I Was in The War: Experiences of Coventry Men in the Great War', 1937–1938

Heap, Arthur, Newspaper Cuttings, 1915–1920

Midland Daily Telegraph, 1914–1920

The Coventrian, magazine of King Henry VIII School, 1915–1925

The Limit, magazine of White and Poppe Ltd, 1918–1920

The Rudge Record, magazine of Rudge Whitworth and Co. 1914–1915

The Wheatleyan, magazine of Bablake School, 1911–1919

Vita Nuova, magazine of Barr's Hill School, 1912–1928

Books

Beaven, Brad, *Leisure, Citizenship and Working Class Men in Britain 1850–1945* (Manchester University Press, 2005)

Freeman, Tony, *Humber 1868–1976: An Illustrated History* (Yesteryear Books, 1991)

Harkin, Trevor, *City of Coventry Roll of the Fallen: The Great War* (War Memorial Park Publications, 2009)

Hodgkinson, George, *Sent to Coventry* (Robert Maxwell & Co., 1970)

Holland, Chris (ed.), *Coventry and Warwickshire 1914–1919: Local aspects of the Great War* (Warwickshire Great War Publications, Volumes One and Two, 2012/2014)

Holland, Chris (ed.), *The 29th Division in Warwickshire and North Oxfordshire December 1914 – March 1915* (Warwickshire Great War Publications, 2014)

Holland, Chris and Phillips, Rob (eds), *The Great War Letters of Roland Mountford* (Matador, 2009)

Hotchkiss, *Souvenir of the Hotchkiss Works* (1922)

Hunt, Cathy, *The National Federation of Women Workers 1906–1921* (Palgrave Macmillan, 2014)

Lancaster, Bill, and Mason, Tony (eds), *Life & Labour in a 20th Century City* (University of Warwick, 1985)

McGrory, David, *Around Coventry in Old Photographs* (Alan Sutton Publishing, 1991)

The Women's Research Group, *Against All Odds* (2011)

The Work of the Daimler Company in the First World War (1921)

Walters, Peter, *The Story of Coventry* (The History Press, 2013)

Wilkins, Henry Charles, *Journal of the European War 1914–1918* (1919)

Yates, John, *Pioneers to Power* (Coventry Labour Party, 1950)

Journals and Other Sources

Batchelor, Lawrence Anthony, *A Great Munitions Centre: Coventry's Armaments and Munitions Industry 1914–1918* (Coventry University Master's Degree, 2008)

Coventry Chamber of Commerce Journal 1914–1915

Reports of Coventry and Warwickshire Hospital 1912–1915

Reports of Coventry's Chief Constable 1914–1918

Reports of Coventry's Chief Medical Officer 1914–1918

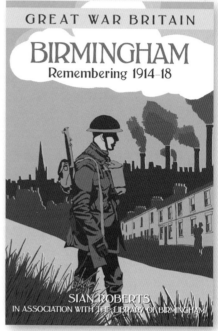